The Chaos of Being Kyle

A Mental Health Story

Kyle Jensen

Dedication

To my wife, Jordan, you came into my life at God's right time. Your love and compassionate heart help me to get through every day. You have always believed in me and made me want to do better. God truly gave me you for the ups and downs!

To my late father, Glen, I hope to have made you proud looking down from heaven. It was always my aspiration to be successful in your eyes.

To my mom Barbara, you gave and instilled in me heavenly tools that are invaluable. You never gave up on me in tough times, and that is a sign of true love.

To my brother Erik, I have always looked up to you and have been proud to be your brother. I will never forget the time and effort you spent when I was sick to ensure I would get better. Thank you.

Acknowledgments

To all those that struggle with a mental ailment, I hear you; I see you, and I feel your pain. May God be with you until we can be 'normal' again.

To those who have ever been affected by domestic violence, don't be afraid to seek out help. It is not your fault. You deserve better.

For all my amazing teachers, coaches, and professors, Thanks for mentoring me, investing in me, and taking the time to see the worth in me, even at times when I did not find it in myself.

For all my potential readers, I hope this book can be useful to you, and I hope it can be something of value to your life.

CONTENTS

PART 1

Foreword

This short biographical story is about the life, struggles, and tribulations of myself Kyle Jensen. My memoir's purpose is to shed light on mental health, God's grace, and how love conquers all. Without the Lord, I would not be alive. I would have committed suicide long ago due to years of struggling with a multitude of traumas. Many people feel that individuals with bipolar are violent, which is a common misconception. In my perception, some folks think a person who has bipolar disorder or schizophrenia can just go crazy at the drop of a coin. Although it happens occasionally, for the most part, it is not true. To make matters worse, in my situation, I am around 360 pounds. Not only am I rowdy when I am manic, but I can also elevate my voice. The loud volume causes others to be in a state of fear. However, their concern is unfounded. Manic or not, I am the gentlest person you will ever have the grace of meeting. I have been on record crying when I saw a toad killed on the side of the road.

I just wanted to point out that people perceive bipolar or schizophrenic individuals as a threat. Most, if not all of us, are pretty peaceful. I would compare us to a snake. We will not attack unless directly threatened. In my opinion, some people deserve to be talked to in a forceful manner, such as with profanity, because they must be educated. For instance, someone at a pizza restaurant near our house told me they did not have my order. He explained to me that I must have ordered at the place across town. Without hesitation, I asked for his manager while saying some four-letter words. As you might have guessed, the missing food showed up three seconds later. The mishap was just pure laziness on the employee's part.

Throughout my life, God's grace, and his eternal plan, helped me through several trials and misfortunes. My story is far from over. In fact, as a thirty-two-year-old, it is still on the rise. Sometimes I just have to let go and let God take care of my situation. When I was in high school, if someone wronged me, I went for revenge. As an adult, I know that the best way to get back at a jerk is to walk away. Eventually, karma will take care of them. Through all my struggles and mental challenges, there was always a way to cope. As the old Greek myth goes, the only thing left in Pandora's box after the evil came out was hope!

Chapter 1
Getting Sick at Seventeen

When I was seventeen, I got sick with severe depression. Nothing could make me happy. I had always had a larger-than-life, extroverted personality. A great example of my confidence would be how I sang the national anthem before class every single day during my senior year. I was a defensive back on the football team. Though other classmates were more popular than me, I still had a lot of friends.

In November 2006, my girlfriend at the time had just broken up with me. We will call her Rachel. The two of us had been dating for three months. I would spend the night at her house almost every weekend. My parents were unaware of our alone time because one of my best friends lived right next to her. Instead of going to his place like I told my mom and dad, I would stay at hers. We had an okay relationship. It was filled with many good times, but we were not the right fit. I was moping around daily at my parents' house, licking my wounds. On a rough evening, after my ex had ended things, I had gone to a party at a friend's home in our neighborhood in Chester, Arkansas, and hooked up with three different girls, beyond intoxicated for most of the gathering.

We hung out, drank, and partied well into the night. My drinking began a tailspin.

On my way coming home one day, I thought my tires were slashed. If I was thinking logically, how could I have driven on ripped tires? However, I literally ran my fingers through the gashes. It would be like saying the sky was blue; that is how real it was to me. My mom compared my delusions to that of me seeing a dinosaur. I honestly saw the creature even though I knew it did not exist. Soon after, I lost forty pounds in one month due to my severe depression. School, which was once my favorite to go to, had become a chore. It was hard for me to eat, listen, and even articulate a sentence, let alone write down my name.

The counselors at my high school could tell something was wrong. With my mother's blessing, all my teachers called an emergency meeting. They could see my weight had drastically changed. The instructors were used to my strong, confident, borderline cocky persona. I was but a shell of myself, saying erroneous things that just never happened. I thought I had done stuff that actually had not occurred. Anyone and everyone could tell I needed help.

One of my English teachers told my mom I could not even remember my name. My mother had no other choice but for me to see my primary care physician. He prescribed me an antidepressant that doctors are not supposed to give to minors. The drug just exacerbated matters. I was on the brink of suicide. My thought process was I would either die from not eating or drinking or maybe even taking my life. One day, my mom made me a burger. She wept as she noticed I would not eat it. Was I hungry? Of course, but I was too far gone. So, my mother stepped in, realizing hospitalization was my only option.

Going to Mercy Hospital, I was scared to death. The car ride seemed to last a long time, even though traffic was light. When we made it to the hospital, my family asked me to step out of the vehicle. I was too scared to budge. Resisting their requests, I wedged my leg into the seat, and security had to force me out of the automobile. After they got me settled inside the facility, I stood in a secluded room, not blinking or even flinching, for an hour straight. It was as if I was a tree that could not move. In my delusional mind, I thought they were going to kill me. Upon arriving at the medical center, I was dehydrated enough that the doctors gave me four bags of IV fluids. The staff informed my family that I needed food. They force-fed me a burger, and it was off to Victory Hospital I went. My stay at Mercy was so short because the doctors and nurses figured the other location had the personnel and medicine necessary to treat me.

Chapter 2

How the Symptoms Started

So, bipolar is typically hereditary. For me, it was just a matter of time before it would manifest. At seventeen, I was a fearless individual. Hell, I was voted the most talkative out of my whole class. It all began when I went to consult the dentist to get my wisdom teeth. They gave me a steroid that would make things worse in my life. I started getting sick, and my outspoken demeanor turned quickly. I could not spell my name most of the time. Being a student who got As and Bs, my grades also suffered. Worse still, my sleep was nonexistent. It was documented that I stopped sleeping for a week straight. I needed help in the direst way. Remember that illegal drug my primary care physician gave me? Well, it sure made me go to bed at night. I was knocked out for what felt like years. My symptoms unfortunately continued, and I begged my parents for help.

Chapter 3
First Victory Hospital Trip

My parents were convinced that taking me to Victory Hospital was the right first step. The workers there seemed to be sweet toward my mom and dad and did genuinely seem to care about my health. It was tough being a young buck in there with mental health issues when most patients were older and more aggressive than me.

Most of the young men in there had issues with drugs and violence and had been repeated juvenile offenders. There was one Hispanic kid who constantly picked on me. He would insult me, tell me I looked like a zombie, and push me around. The dude told me to call him the muffin man. Still, to this day, I do not know what that means. I remember sleeping most of the time. In fact, I forgot how to walk around because I was in bed so much. I remember taking a brain test in a separate facility where all such assessments took place. To me, it felt like electric shock therapy, but that was probably just my mind. We took tests on geography on multiple occasions. I always scored high on the state capital ones. Math was another story. I could not remember simple numbers. My family visited me like clockwork, and my parents were there early and often. Even though my brother was working and going to school full-time, he never missed a session. That meant the world to me! I will never forget his kindness and acts of love. I am forever indebted to him. My stay lasted around two months because I had to gain a certain amount of weight before leaving. The staff gave me a thick weight gainer. I went from 140 pounds to around 210 in just two months. People in the facility were decently nice there, but it was time for me to go home.

Chapter 4
Better, at Least for Now

Two months after first arriving at the hospital, I felt like I was getting better. My mom and dad picked me up. Even though I was lethargic, on the inside, I only experienced joy. They brought with them my favorite pizza from the local restaurant I loved the most. My parents also got me a soda from a gas station and my favorite candy. The food was not horrible at the hospital, but the eats they provided were better. Mom and dad made sure I was happy and the healthiest I had been in a while. Boy, was I glad to be home. Even hearing our older pup bark made me at ease. It was time to try and go back to school.

The Alma, Arkansas School District allowed me two options. I could take an online course to make up for my missed time, or I could reenroll in courses. I chose the latter. It was weird returning to class for the first time after being sick. Students and teachers alike were looking at me like I was crazy. Rumors were swirling around that I had been in a mental institution. It got so bad that one classmate of mine asked me if I had gone "psycho." High school students can be so cruel. I know from experience because I was that kid. I was the one who would make fun of you, belittle you, and make you cry. Educators were not immune from my narcissistic tendencies. I brutally made fun of a science teacher one day, and she left the room weeping. What kind of a man was I? Hardly one at all, I would say.

I only needed two more courses to graduate—one English and one elective. After leaving Victory, I received treatment from Dr. Gary (not that that is his real name). He was a strange individual in general. He never seemed focused and was always looking all over the place. When he would look at me directly, it was like he was constantly taking the time to weigh my good traits against my bad ones. I always thought something was a little off with him. However, I have been told you have to be a little weird to be a psychological doctor. During one session, he called me "arrogant" because I wore sunglasses inside his office building. I was unaware then that doing so was a sign of thinking highly of yourself. We did not get along, and eventually, he took me off all my medicine and discharged me completely from his outpatient department. Three months later, I heard he had committed suicide. Upon discovering the news, my heart was heavy. Apparently, he was having problems of his own. His wife was seeing someone behind his back. Tragically, he killed the two of them and himself in a vicious double homicide/suicide. Yet I was the one who had a psychosis. What a shame!

Chapter 5

Second Victory Hospital Visit

In July 2007, I got into a horrible car accident. I was on the way to see my girlfriend and was driving way too fast. There was only one thing on my brain: wanting to sleep with her. Weeks before, we had gotten it on in a retail parking lot in the middle of the day. That crazed act had me thinking about her constantly. I was driving around twenty-five miles over the limit. To me, the other car was coming into my lane. I swerved to miss the approaching vehicle and went into a ravine. I busted my windshield completely and felt a presence come over me. My windshield was caved in, yet I did not hit my head against it. The guy who almost hit me came running down and asked if I was fine. Only the backseat served as an exit because the front was impassible. When I got up to the highway, a police officer arrived on the scene.

I still remember him saying, "Where is the dead body?" To which I exclaimed, "I'm still alive." My poor mother got there just a little later. She immediately wept and praised God that I was still breathing. As she yelled at me to get on my knees and thank the Lord, I felt shards of glass scrape against my legs. Though there was not heavy bleeding, it was not pleasant. The officer gave me a ticket for careless driving and sent me to a class for people to relearn the rules of the road.

Months passed, and I went to the University of Arkansas–Fort Smith for college. I did not know what I was doing or how difficult classes would be. It was so bad that my grades dropped. My athletic ability led me to constantly miss class, which did not help. Hell, I was even a decent ping-pong player. To make matters worse, I got into two altercations and had to see the dean as many times. For the first fight, a guy made fun of me and got in my face. I told him he looked like a billy goat and that I would beat his ass. He was an extremely shaggy dude. The second was with my brother. We were playing flag football, and things got heated. My brother told me I was not trying during the first half of the game. I proceeded to try to take a nap. The next thing I knew, he was punching me in the face. The referees broke us up, and the police were called. The officer on duty asked me if I wanted to press charges, but I declined. I struggled in my classes, making Cs in several and failing college algebra. Things were just not going well for me that first semester.

I decided to take up mixed martial arts after watching the Ultimate Fighting Championship on TV. I drove all the way from Chester to Waldron, Arkansas, an eighty-minute drive just to train for half an hour. The trip there took so long because I decided not to live in the dorms. My delusions were starting to happen. I told people I had a record of five and zero and other lies. One day driving back from Waldron, I ran out of gas. My parents had to come to my aid.

In October 2007, I got sick again. This time, it was somewhat my fault. I was taking Hydroxycut Hardcore to get better results on army fitness tests, and somehow, I had an adverse reaction. Joining the army was always something I yearned to do. I endured months of clearance checks just to be able to enlist. This was due to my previous psychiatric history. My recruiter assured me I would be taken care of. A few weeks later, the army made their decision. I was leaving for basic training in January 2008. Little did I know that was not my destiny.

The Hydroxycut made me think I was the archangel Michael and was to bring judgment on people for their sins. Out of nowhere, I moved in with my bunkmate and his family. We lived right across the street from a church. His mother and father eventually kicked me out of the house. They knew I was having delusions, and it was time for me to leave. My mom told me I could come home. It was noon when my friend's parents and I started having an argument. Our words were done at about three in the afternoon. I made the parallel to when Jesus died on the cross around the same time. I was away from my parents for a week. When I got home, I told my dad I was an archangel and to cut me because I would not bleed. Of course, he refused. My parents were informed of my diet pill use. Together, we burned the pills. They assumed my delusions would stop. Trouble was, they did not.

Next was the Christmas service. I volunteered to read a scripture passage. I helped an older lady get from her chair to the back and sang my heart out. While I was singing, I remember our pastor saying, "Kyle of Chester," in the way they would have said, "Jesus of Nazareth." So, I told my parents I really was Michael. My dad got angry and pushed me, which caused me to push him back harder. He was silent because he did not know what I was capable of. My dear parents begged me to go to Mercy Hospital. I agreed to head there with them to get treatment. While in a room by myself, I heard a voice saying I needed to save the world. I got on my stomach (on the floor) and said a prayer. While I was praying, I felt the Lord tell me I was going to be okay. Minutes later, an attractive doctor came to my room. She gave me breakfast and left a note that said, "Enjoy your breakfast. Love God." Though this was a hallucination, it was clear as day to me at the time. They eventually had to take me to the mental hospital.

Unfortunately, I was getting mistreated in solitary confinement. The abuses angered me, and I told the staff I was going to bust down the door. Naturally, they called the police, and what happened next would stay with me forever. Seven people had me cornered in a room. I eventually gave myself up. The cops cuffed me, but I was still a little mouthy to them. The officer put all his weight on my neck and uttered profanities that should never be spoken to anyone. Since my adrenaline was at an all-time high, I told him to get off me, and if he did not, I would break the handcuffs and make him feel sorry. The female officer seemed to be the voice of reason. She calmed both of us down and humored me by saying I was the archangel, Michael.

She said she believed me. Several minutes later, I finally relaxed, and everyone left the room. I was in full-blown mania again the next day. With my adrenaline in hyperdrive, I tried to escape by the steel door in the hallway. I wanted nothing more than to get out of the hospital. To my shock, five Victory workers pinned me up against the wall and injected me with medicine. Two minutes later, I was out cold. I came to my senses just a little later and saw a young staff member who was making me tea. For the purpose of the story, the man's name will be Steven. In my delusional state, I thought he was the devil. I could see him as Lucifer himself. I took the glass he gave to me for drinking and poured it all over his clothes. That stunt put me back in solitary confinement for the rest of the week. Another worker, who will be called Janet, befriended me. She told me everything was going to be all right. She was doing my laundry and even sneaked me a meal from the outside. I had a vision that Janet was supposed to be my wife when I took over the world as Michael. Throughout the facility, everyone knew me as a prophet. My bravado grew each day.

Later that month, I had my day in court. My parents had filed a petition for me to go to the courthouse itself. I was put in shackles and driven to the Crawford County courthouse to attend a hearing. It was probably the toughest moment of my life to see my mom in tears pleading with the court to help me. I was committed for forty-five days. During my hearing, I told a lady I would defend her as her lawyer. Let us face facts. I was out of my mind. The police officer who took me in started to make fun of me. How cruel can one be? Eventually, I would get out of Victory. For a couple of weeks, a patient advocate was trying to find me a place to stay. I was called to Russellville.

Chapter 6
The Russellville Facility

I spent seven months in what I will call the
Russellville facility. When I got to the place, I was in
tip-top shape. I left overweight, sad, and a little bit
nervous about things to come. Upon arrival, I met a
young kid who had court-ordered to be there. It was
evident he was obese. I used to rub his belly. By the
end of my time there, I was bigger than he was. It was
good getting to know people in the in-home facility.
Fifteen other people lived with me there. Most of them
were felons, and some were just in there for other
reasons. There was a dentist there who, due to mental
health issues, lost his temper. There was also a worker;
we will call her Anna, who loved me like I was her own
son. She was a friend among strangers. What a lovely
woman! I was constantly telling people about my
archangel position. One man bowed to me because he
believed in me so much. I would yell outside, and the
ground would echo. One day, I went to get my driver's

license renewed with the staff. During that errand, I told the department of motor vehicles worker that I was in a witness protection program and asked her if my status would affect my renewal.

There was a girl who borderline became obsessed with me. Plot twist: she thought she was an angel too. One day, my family came to visit me. Things were okay, but my life could have been better. All my delusions were still present. I remember this one lady in the facility who drank only mountain dew. I kid you not; she looked exactly like a witch. Since I was eighteen in those days, I longed for home. Thankfully, I made a friend in that facility who will be called Robert. He was a sweet man and always wanted to play PlayStation with me. He made the days go by faster. It took a lot of prayers, help from my doctors, and medicine to break me from my delusions.

When April rolled around, I took a new drug called Invega. From that moment on, I never thought I was Michael again. Although I was better, it was the biggest letdown imaginable. Can you comprehend thinking you hold all the power in the world for six months, then one day it is gone? They released me to go home with my family in July.

Chapter 7
Mountainburg Struggles

Coming out of the hospital, I rented an apartment in Mountainburg to be near my parents. Initially, I was ecstatic to be home. My joy was short-lived because I fell into a dark place. I was depressed, did not have a car, and barely had any social life. Things were looking bleak. The only sort of happiness I experienced was my weekly grocery trips with my mother. Even those did not make me content. All things considered, I was down on my luck. Few people visited me outside of my one or two friends. At one point, I contemplated taking my own life. As I picked up a knife, I prayed and told God to help me. Of course, the Lord works in mysterious ways, and without delay, a bird came to my window and started singing. It was as if God said, "This is my child!" I continued to pray. Things would eventually get better.

Chapter 8
College

I went back to our local university from 2009 to 2013. I dated a young lady who, for the story's purpose, will be called Avery. At the time of our meeting, I was taking one class per semester. My pace meant I would have needed twelve years to graduate. She pushed me to be better academically. I eventually took more and more credit hours, culminating at seventeen from my sophomore year until graduation. From listening to Avery, my degree only took four years. One major takeaway from college came during my commencement ceremony. I had five different instructors come up to me and tell me I had done a great job. Then there was my cum laude status and 3.77-grade point average, ranking me second in my class of 180 people. My major was organizational leadership. To this day, I am not sure what the degree is really made for. It is broad-based, however, and has provided several job and networking opportunities.

Before and after college, it was hard for me to keep a job. I would move from one position to the next but never settle down in a career. I chuckle when I hear that some people have had three jobs their whole life. I have had three in a matter of two weeks. Throughout my life, I have held more than sixty. My illness was a contributing factor holding me back. Something would always upset me, and I played the victim card well. I was fired from a sporting goods store for sleeping in the boating section. A couple of months later, I got terminated from the movie theater for fighting with a coworker. My relationship with Avery was decent. She was a sweet, kind nurse who cared about me deeply. Many times, she missed work to take care of me, and she always had my best interest at heart.

It worked both ways, as she would have panic attacks because of the difficulty of nursing school. I actually took a couple of classes for her because she did not have enough time. She was there for me through a plethora of different situations. For instance, I had a car accident one morning on the way to my clerical job. I went through a green light and T-boned a young man who ran a red light. After hitting him, my car bounced off right into another vehicle. The other person I had hit was taken to the hospital because of their injuries. This accident caused me to have several panic attacks almost every day, like clockwork. Avery supported me in any way she could, even taking off work. I could not get my mind right after the incident. I got stressed over the littlest things. It was my illness consuming me. One day, Avery lost her keys. As a result, I had to take her thirty minutes to work and be late myself. We could not find her keys for two days. I called her irresponsible and told her she needed to get it together. On the second day, I stumbled around and kicked a shoe. The jingle that came from the shoe helped us locate the keys.

Although we seemed like a power couple, we bickered a lot. It was mostly over her sleep schedule. She would go to bed past two in the morning and wake up sometimes twelve hours later. In May 2015, we went on a cruise to save our relationship, but it had the opposite effect. I saw her for the lazy, lethargic person she was. Unfortunately, our spark was gone.

Soon after college, I took a position as a supervisor of a disabilities work facility. Though I did not agree with what the workers were paid, it was still a fulfilling role. One of my subordinate's employees at the job, however, was texting me inappropriate things. Regrettably, I did not stop her advances. She asked me to go to the park with her, and I ended up agreeing. Although, nothing really happened. The woman did touch me improperly, and I was anxious I would get in trouble because of it. Even though I did not do anything, I was her direct supervisor, after all. My boss caught wind, and we had a meeting. Several people were interviewed, but nothing came of it which cleared my name.

Though we did get engaged, my relationship with Avery fell apart because of persistent lying on my end. She and I eventually broke up due to me being unfaithful—fitting how a lack of judgment can result in a terrible situation. It all happened when Avery went to Russellville to visit her sister. Due to our failed relationship, and lack of control, I went to a young lady's house to party. I met her, a cute blonde, at her apartment. She was fully aware that I was engaged, but that did not seem to deter her. We started doing yoga, and one thing led to another. I ended up sleeping with her but was so appalled and ashamed of my actions that I immediately asked God for his forgiveness. Through prayer, he told me Avery needed to know. I told her, which quickly ended the relationship. After, I moved in with a friend from church. Avery and I met up one last time at a local retail store to exchange our things. We talked for just a couple of minutes, and I could tell she was taking the break hard. I remember her putting her head on the steering wheel of her car and weeping profusely. The woman I had loved for six years was in incredible pain. Cheating on her and ending the relationship terribly remain some of my

biggest regrets.

Chapter 9
My Father's Passing

My father and I had a relationship like good friends. He was a disciplined, intelligent man who gave wonderful advice. To say I adored my dad's intelligence and education would be an understatement. I truly believe he was one of the most brilliant people I have ever met. He had his MBA. He decided to dropout out of junior high in ninth grade, but due to his stepfather's urging, he got his GED. After that came his undergraduate and graduate degrees. There was no denying his humor, love of music, and appreciation for nature. Dad would frequently listen to Alanis Morrisette, Tom Petty, and Ozzy Osbourne. He taught me that it was truly possible to be huntin', fishin', and lovin' every day. My father loved the woods and the river. He was a big-game hunter who killed a grizzly bear, mountain goat, black bear, turkey, and antelope, to name a few.

When I was in eighth grade, he and I went to British Columbia to hunt mountain goats. Dad killed his early on and decided to go fishing the rest of the time, leaving me with the guide. I missed my opportunity at a huge Billy Goat. I remember going to see my dad back at the guide's house and apologizing for letting him down by returning with nothing. He told me he loved me, and we embraced. It was the most intimate moment we would spend together, and I will never forget it.

Later that year, dad and I went to hunt deer at Fort Chaffee back in Arkansas. At around noon, I heard a lot of rustling in the woods. I figured it was lunch time since my father wanted me to come to him. I called out his name on more than two occasions, but no one responded. Looking offer my left shoulder, I spotted a huge, ten-point buck. I got my bearings and shot the animal. My dad must have heard the shot or been close by because he came immediately. We looked for the deer and found a blood trail. My shot had impacted the deer's windpipe. My father exclaimed, "Is this your deer? Is this your deer?" I would imagine it was the proudest he had ever been of me.

There were also our family trips to Roaring River State Park in Missouri. Though I did not appreciate it then, it was good to spend so much time with my loved ones. I remember dad saving a young girl's life. She had drifted off to asleep and fallen into a fire. Without skipping a beat, he pulled her out, sparing her from fatal injury.

During my younger years, my dad missed many of my school functions, and I longed for his attention. I was a successful athlete in little league basketball, but he did not see most of my achievements. While I was in ninth grade, things changed. The man turned from being a cold father to a loving, caring family man. It had to have been God doing wonderful things for him and his desire to be closer to the Lord. My father had seen my struggles. He knew how painful it was for me and my mom. The first time I went to the hospital, he was willing to lose his job just so he could be by my side.

Dad was always a cigarette smoker and coffee drinker. I used to fake a cough so he would stop smoking. He picked up on it and was not happy. He had a stressful job, which had him working around the clock. I was always extremely proud of my father's determination since it is a shared trait. Through many situations, we have been resilient in the face of trials.

My father developed a cough of his own and went to the doctor. I talked to him about finances one day in the basement of the family house. He broke down in tears, and I feared the worst. My dad was diagnosed with cancer in 2016. Trying to avoid the situation, I fled to Conway, Arkansas, a town about two hours away. My wife at the time kept me from my father. She did this because she did not want my mood to change. Dad's cancer got progressively worse. Given that he was one smart cookie, he knew my spouse was not the one for me. I just could not see the truth myself.

One January morning, my mom called me when I was working at Allstate and told me my dad was about to die. I knew it was time. I returned to Chester in what seemed like minutes. Forty minutes later, Glen Jensen had passed. I would give anything to hear his voice one more time, to heed his advice, to hug him, to hunt with him. Hell, just being in his presence would be enough. Luckily, my father was a God-fearing man and is with the Almighty.

After, the family had to pay their respects. However, there were challenges right off the bat. My ex-wife decided it would be acceptable to make a social media post stating my dad said a lot of sexual innuendos. I was mortified. She just was not much of a thinker when it came to other people's feelings. The funeral came and went. I tried holding it together during the service but started crying when I heard

"Amazing Grace." We buried my dad, and it was time to grieve.

Chapter 10
Whom Did I Marry?

I met Terry, though that is not her actual name, on a social media website. One afternoon, I messaged two girls, and she was the only one who responded. We had a topsy-turvy relationship. One day would be good, while the next would be bad. When I met her, I worked at the local church doing clerical work and was living with a friend from the same place. Terry would come over, and we would sleep together. Our closeness did not sit well with my Christian roommate, and he told me I needed to make a choice between living with my girlfriend or him. I left his house that day. One month later, Terry and I moved in together. Two months after we first started dating, I got an interview as a program director of a trade school.

Though I had minimal experience, my interview went well. I was offered the job, which was fifty minutes away. The position gave me an eight-dollar raise from my post at the parish, so I thought I had to take it. After asking the pastor of the church if he could match the competing salary, he simply offered a whopping twenty-five cent raise, meaning it was time for me to go. My new career drove a wedge in my relationship with Terry because I was gone all the time. It did not help that the teachers and other women going to the school would constantly flirt with me. What can I say? The babes loved me. Shortly after dating, we got engaged. I still think I gave her the sweetest marriage proposal. I took her to five places as a scavenger hunt for the memories of our relationship.

First was when I brought her best friend from up north down to meet her at the movies. Then her brother was at an ice cream place (our first dessert). Her dad was at a retail shop (first shopping trip). Fourth was the local lake where she met my best friend, Jimmy (when I showed her my feelings for her). The proposal ended with me on one knee and with two rings, one for Terry and one for her daughter

Catherine. We got married in 2016 for insurance purposes. She had diabetes, and her testing supplies were outrageously expensive. To make matters worse, Terry was abusive. The day after saying our vows, we got into an argument.

She kicked me out of her car, forcing me to walk three miles home at night. That day, I asked her for a divorce. It did not matter to me that our marriage was so young. Things were already unpleasant. Eventually, the abuse turned physical. She hit me on more than four occasions. I knew she was violent based on how she reacted when I saved Catherine from a dog attack. After the rescue, I returned to the house, but the neighbors were talking ill of me. Terry said she would handle the situation and went out to confront them. She told them if they ever talked bad about me, she would kill them. Her brother was also violent.

The abuse started off as verbal in nature. You would think that would be easier to handle, but it was worse, to be honest. When we first met, I was in the best shape of my life. I had a legit six-pack, and I would always say I was ripped like Rambo. She was extremely attracted to me, as were most of her friends. One day while training for a half-marathon, I felt a burning sensation in my hamstring. It was just my luck; I was only on mile six of a session that lasted ten. Stupidly, I finished the race with a torn hamstring. An MRI revealed it was a complete tear. The doctor said surgery was possible, but I decided against it and thus could not work out for two months. Due to depression, I gained around fifteen pounds, which prompted Terry to call me fat frequently.

She would constantly touch and pat my stomach. She was skinny, but she was clearly out of shape. Given my training, I could run many miles at a time, while she would get winded after a quarter mile. Soon, Terry started using other insults. She would call me stupid constantly. It was ironic, considering she barely passed her GED as a high school dropout, and I was a decorated college graduate. Some of our other fights always seemed to end with me getting thrown out of the car. One day, Terry made me get out after we had an argument going through a drive-through. I ran five miles home in jeans. I also remember running out of gas at a retail store. I asked her to bring me the debit card I had forgotten at home. It was a hot summer day and a heated exchange. She yelled at me, told me I was stupid, gave me the card, and left. My only option was to walk two miles in the scorching heat to get gas and just as many back.

Her brother Larry—also a fake name—and I started off as close friends. Both were dealing with mental health issues, and we bonded. We would watch football together, play sports, and just have a good time. He was schizophrenic and was off his medicine for several weeks. One day, he called Terry. He said he was going to kill me. Not listening to my advice, she went and stood up to him. Larry proceeded to get more violent. He had a baseball bat with him, which scared me. To make matters worse, Terry got in his face and he pushed her. After the police got involved, he was strapped into an ambulance. Restraining him was a mistake because he escaped from the straps and broke the paramedic's nose. Consequently, he did four months of jail time. When he got out, you could tell he was a little loopy. His actions probably contributed to my mania as well.

His threats and arrest troubled me. One day, I locked myself in my apartment because I thought he was going to come to attack me. My mind was playing tricks on me. Thankfully, he never did. Larry and I would eventually get back on good terms. We even traveled five hours to go to a playoff basketball game.

Terry and I had quite a strange relationship. There were so many moments where crap hit the fan. I called her a name one night, and she got the biggest butcher knife in the house and stuck it to my throat. She said, "Say that name again, and I will kill you." The next moment of abuse was when she choked me so hard I blacked out. She was not done with mistreating me. I told her again one morning that I wanted a divorce. She hit me in the face four times, giving me somewhat of a black eye. After, she got into a defensive stance and headbutted me. We both cried profusely. Why did I stay so long? I mean, the situation was obviously abusive. Well, I just wanted a family and to be loved. I also adored her little girl Catherine, and I yearned for the girl to have a good life.

Catherine's biological father was a real winner. He won himself eight felonies due to drugs, gun charges, and other crimes. He and I had a few incidents with each other. When I first met him, he tried to intimidate me by getting in my face with a group of friends. He wanted me to know Terry and her house were his territory and even went on to say she was his "property." Another time, we went to drop off Catherine for a visit and smelled alcohol on his breath. He was obviously drunk off his butt. I told Terry we should not leave her daughter with a criminal. She informed me the court had given him some visitation rights. Catherine's father paid a whopping eighty-seven dollars every eight months for child support. He was in debt of at least fifteen thousand in paying to support his daughter.

Yet through all this, his daughter thought he was the greatest person alive. What Catherine failed to realize was that I was the one taking care of her. Though not her father by blood, I was her dad in every other sense of the word. I took her to school, went to all parent-teacher conferences, and took off work to watch her sing in plays. I loved Catherine as if she was my own kid. At some points, however, I had to be the disciplinarian. For instance, on a trip to the pharmacy to pick up my medicine, Catherine asked for a toy. I told her she could not have it. This was a cold, wintery day, mind you, and I saw that her jacket looked quite larger than before. I asked her if she had something stuffed in it. She had the toy! We were already in the car, and I was mortified. I immediately had her walk with me and tell the manager herself that she had taken the item. Catherine loved me and saw me as a dad. Heck, she called me daddy after one month of being with her mother. Terry and I were on the brink of a breakup one day. Catherine ran out to my car and prevented me from leaving. My favorite story of her was when we took the girl to the dentist for the first time. The hygienist asked who she wanted to sit in on the appointment. Her exact words were, "My daddy! He will protect me."

Another negative aspect of our marriage was the poor choices my ex-wife made. She would frequently party into the wee hours of the night, which was tough for someone who has type 1 diabetes. Partying was not my scene, so I just stayed home and watched her daughter while she had a good time. Terry also smoked a lot of marijuana. Almost every day, she hit the bong. My ex-wife did drag me out to one of her best friend's themed parties. It was going okay until the cocaine came out. Everyone in the entire house started doing lines. When I refused, they made fun of me. Not only was coke new to me, but I was also scared we were going to get caught and I would go to jail just for being there. It was time to leave. So, I went to the backyard and started walking. Higher than a plane, she eventually caught up to me. Terry said she was embarrassed by me. I told her she was a sorry excuse for a mother. An argument ensued, but all was not lost...yet.

I ended up getting my dream job with a big insurance firm. They needed me to train in a different state and would pay for my meals and lodging. Right before I left for the position, I went to get Terry a coffee from a local shop. My plan was to return in ten minutes. Unfortunately, I never made it back home. I went to a gas station and was a little agitated. The clerk asked me if I wanted to gamble. Why not? My first scratcher yielded me five hundred dollars. I was hooked and continued to buy out the store. I thought I would get my money back eventually, but it never happened. After losing $1,200 initially, I over drafted and lost another five hundred. I went straight to work and, on the way, turned my phone off. Terry called my mother, and I was in trouble with both women. Mom was sweet enough to pay our rent that month so we could avoid eviction.

There was infidelity on both sides. When I was training for an insurance position, she was sleeping with a guy seven years younger than her. I, myself, was no saint, given my affair with one of my coworkers. Terry would frequently call, and I would send her straight to voicemail. I could not blame her for cheating. Even though I did invite her out for the weekend a few times, Terry never visited me those two months I was out of state training.

During my time away, my mania came out to play once again. Insomnia ensued. I remember one day, after a tough work shift, I got into it with one of my coworkers. She explained to me how she was the better salesperson. For one reason or another, her claim struck a nerve. Instead of taking the company shuttle,

I walked five miles on the interstate to get back to the hotel. I would frequently play basketball late into the night, sleep two hours, and run for the same amount of time. The word "rest" was not in my vernacular.

The hotel I was staying at asked me to pay a ten-dollar deposit for incidentals two weeks after being there. I told them I did not have that at the time, which was mostly due to my previous gambling. They informed me I had to leave and would not even let me back to my room to get my belongings. As soon as I called my company, it was taken care of. They resolved it because of the copious amount of money they spent on hotels.

After returning from training, my relationship tanked. My ex-wife and I fought every day. We were mostly arguing about me wanting to purchase a home. I thought it was a good investment, but she disagreed. We decided to separate, and she moved in her with her parents. One day, I came over to give Catherine and her three hundred dollars in cash. Her mother exclaimed, "You make more than that!" I told her I was not going to take her abuse, and I collected my things and left. Her brother once again got physical with me. As I was walking away, he pushed me in the back. I told him to stop. He did it again. I yelled at him. He persisted, meaning the fight was on.

It ended with Terry grabbing me by the throat. We went back to our apartment and spent the night together. It all culminated when she had a terrible morning once more. We were arguing severely, and she got a knife and cut her wrist and leg wide open. Her daughter came in and saw she was bleeding on the floor. I had had enough. I felt God urge me to get away. I moved out of the apartment and had nowhere else to stay. Out of options, I lived in a retail parking lot for seven days, still making it to work on time and doing my job. My boss noticed I looked sick. He asked when I last had food. I said four days ago. He immediately bought me lunch. Thankfully, I got enough money to go to a hotel, but it was only temporary. Eventually, I ran out and was homeless again. I got on dating apps and slept with women just to have a place to stay. Life was tough.

Chapter 11
Living in a Parking Lot

After leaving my apartment, I was officially homeless. Having little to no friends in the area, I had to stay in a retailer's parking lot. The vendor allowed semi-trucks to stay there, so it was my best option for residency. It was hot in July 2018. I would guess temperatures rose past one hundred degrees most days. Even though I was hot, tired, and lacked shower facilities, I still went to work every day. My isolation was taking a toll on my mental state. Would things ever turn around?

My situation was also strange. I was in the process of purchasing a house. My loan had been approved for $180,000. All I needed was to close on the property. I kept telling myself I could just be homeless for one more month. Could I have called on my mom for help? Of course. However, I was too prideful.

The Bible talks about how pride comes before the fall, which could not be a more accurate statement. Finally, I got out of that lot. However, it was not the way I wanted to improve my life.

Chapter 12

Abuse at a Medical Center

My mania was getting worse by the day. I got sick one day in Little Rock, and while at the gym thought I ran an unbelievable forty-yard dash time. A young man timed me, and we both agreed his watch was accurate. I was running five hours a day and consistently going on fumes during my shifts. I would need something from a retail shop and decide to run there and back even though it was six miles one way. Delusion affected my work, and I quit my high-paying position with the insurance company. I told my boss I was going to leave and play professional football. After losing my job, I decided it was time to check myself into the hospital. I met a nice guy who will be called Samuel there, and we became best friends. My mom and brother came to visit all the way from Chester. I told my older brother I was a star runner, but he

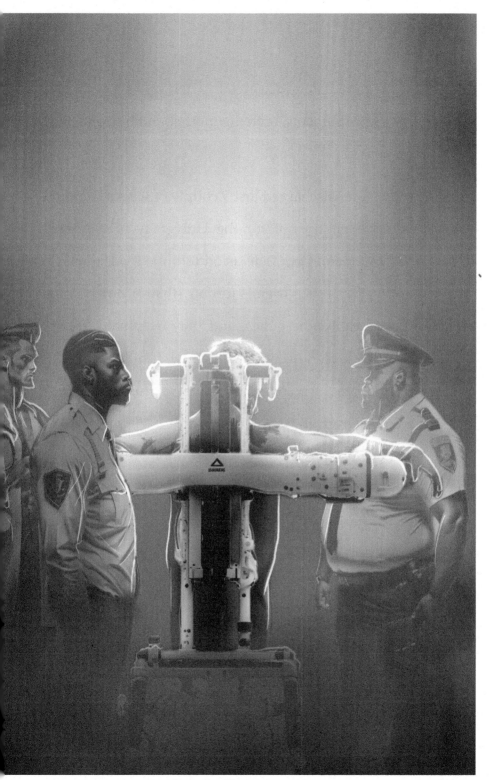

immediately disagreed. After arguing with him for a few moments, both my mother and him had to be dismissed.

I was discharged just a couple of weeks later and went to go try out for the University of Arkansas football team. Or my delusion told me I was going to apply. My other friend, Jordan (that is not his real name), called the police, and they eventually picked me up. I then went to a mental health facility in Springdale, Arkansas. I made a fuss and was frequently given Ativan by the doctors. In fact, I could not even step out of my room without getting a shot. One day, an African American worker was making fun of me hard core. I called him the N-word, and what ensued next was awful.

He got two other black workers and locked the door to my room. Two of them held me down so they could beat me senseless. My nose was dripping blood. After, I was tied down to a large gurney in the shape of a crucifix. The head nurse was in the room with me, though her presence did not have a calming effect. I was getting angrier by the second. My adrenaline had spiked so much that I was starting to lose control. With the added strength, I broke one of the straps and was ready to kill someone. By the grace of God, I caught myself and calmed down. The doctor came in and told me I was a jerk and I should not have used that language. He was right. However, I did not deserve to be abused, put in straps, and made a fool of. I left that facility a couple of days later and returned home to Chester.

Chapter 13

Losing Hope During the Summer of 2018

Finally, I was home. The first night of being back, I went to see my friend, Joey. I had a car but told him I would just walk all the way to his house. After getting lost, my phone died. It was a terrible situation. No hyperbole; I walked all night without stopping. I went through thorns and bled a lot. With a sticky, amber sap on my face, I made it to the local Dollar General fourteen miles away. It was seven in the morning, and the store had just opened. I explained the situation to the workers, and they allowed me to use their cell phones to call my mother. Mom got dressed and picked me up without hesitation. She was worried sick.

Terry came over the next day and asked me if I wanted to drive around in the woods. She had a plan. She wanted to sleep with me. I told her I was hurting but did it anyway. I was cut all over my body from my long walk, but I was also depressed from going through my separation from her. I met up with Terry in the city and received a strange voicemail. I called the number back to find it was Samuel's wife. He had lost his battle with depression and had taken his life. I was devasted and started to cry. Being the apathetic person Terry was, she told me to suck it up and that I barely knew the guy. We went back to her place, and I spent the night. She eventually came over for my birthday in July. Surprisingly, we had a good time. I wept as she drove away. She came back and asked me why I was crying.

I told her it was because I loved her. Then Catherine and she both started tearing up. We did not spend much time together after that. It did not help that she would call me constantly just to spite me. I got wind that she had a live-in boyfriend. I paid her car payment, phone bill, and other fees, all while she was driving to see her partner on my dime with a car in my name; so much for seeing the best in people. Due to all the stress, one afternoon, I took my vehicle to the store. On my way back, I contemplated taking my life and driving off the mountain outside of town. My motive was that my life had nothing anymore. God, however, had other ideas and saved me once again. "How to Save a Life" by the Fray came on the radio at that moment. It sounds unbelievable, but as sure as I am breathing, it happened. I wept and wept and wept some more. The Almighty had saved my life. Praise the Lord.

Chapter 14
New Job, New Me

Save for a couple of short-lived positions over a period of six months; I was jobless. Depression was rearing its ugly head again. I ended up going back to Springdale and getting an interview with a company that, for the sake of the story, will be called Austin Roth Insurance. My interview went well, and I was feeling optimistic about my standing. The owner took a chance on me, and I had a new career and life. I had been going from job to job, but he saw some potential in me. My boss Adam—another fake name—was a joy to work for. Adam and I sold several insurance contracts together, and we had talked about building something special. He even let me rent out a duplex he had. Our business was booming, and we developed a network of several mortgage lenders who would frequently send us referrals. Life and my career were pretty good. I did feel like something was missing. What was it?

Since I could remember, I always wanted to be a college football player. I had always been decently fast, no matter how big I got. My size and speed motivated me to do something strange one afternoon. I called the local high school football coach and asked him if he would time my forty-yard dash. He agreed, and it turned out my run was miserable. I would later recognize it was my lack of faith in the Lord.

Chapter 15
I Am Not Crazy...Well, Maybe I Am

During my episodes, I thought I was an athlete. I think my intense love for sports led to it being my fascination when I experienced mania. It would be commonplace for me to wake up and run every day. Most nights, I would not sleep. My only goal was to run, run, and run. I even went to the insurance office at two in the morning, resting on the floor. Things were getting out of hand. In fact, I ran forty-three miles one day. From two that morning to nine the next, I did not stop. The constant activity caused me to implode. My bipolar was overwhelming me. The writing was on the wall. My struggles kept getting progressively worse.

During that time, I was seeing a new psychiatrist. Making a rookie mistake, she allowed me to control the situation and eventually took me off almost every medicine. Not even two weeks had passed, and I was severely manic. Who did I look to for comfort? I should have sought out the Lord, but I was too far gone.

I was going to a local church and was being prescribed Valium. Apparently, due to my size, I was making people nervous. At this time, I was going to a Men's adult Sunday School class. Due to some members being uneasy, a former cop escorted me to every class I was taking at the church. I was so offended that I decided to quit going to that church altogether.

Chapter 16

I Just Wanted to Be a Pro!

One day, I did not call or show up to work. Instead, I drove to Kansas City to try out for the Chiefs. I left at two in the morning and had a friend send me gas money over Cash App. I was two hours outside of the city when I ran out of gas. I walked two miles to the nearest gas station. I did not have any money and begged a man to give me five dollars. He obliged in exchange for my fifty-inch flat-screen TV. I had no other choice. An hour later, I ran out of gas again and went to find help. Someone called the cops because I was snooping around. I told them I was trying a get a position with the Chiefs. I could tell in the officer's eyes that he knew something was not quite right. I ran out of gas a third time but eventually made it to the stadium. I asked the lady at the ticket office if I could talk to Andy Reid. She told me the guy did not meet with strangers. I then informed her of my five-hour drive. The woman did not understand. There was no way for me to see the coach without an appointment. So, I decided to take matters into my own hands.

I snuck behind the players' practice facility and through the woods. I made it all the way up to the team's locker door when the offensive coordinator walked up and said I could not be there without film or an appointment. I had a long way back home. I made it three hours when, you guessed it, the tank hit empty again. A friend gave me twenty more dollars, and I made it back. Upon returning from Missouri, I went and played basketball at my gym. I was on fire that night. Scoring fourteen of fifteen points for our team, I could not miss. Have you ever heard of Stephen Curry's logo three-point shot? That was exactly what I was doing. From my perspective, stardom was in my future.

The crazy thing about being manic is there is some truth to your delusions. Was I good enough to be a professional basketball player? I would say yes. I am not saying elite but maybe a role player. During manic periods, things come at hyper speed. I can run and think faster, shoot better, and throw farther in basketball. Then there is the increased intelligence. One could compare having mania to the movie Limitless. It is like taking a pill one day and, in the next ten minutes being able to learn languages, understand the stock market, and do things that should not be possible. If only those of us who struggle with mental health could channel the energy.

That early morning, I made forty calls to agents, telling them I was signing with the Oklahoma City Thunder. I had never talked to anyone there despite my convictions. Given my announcement on social media, I thought I had spoken with someone on the team and would be signing with them. The post was met with a substantial amount of criticism. Many people were rude to me. I thought I had a meeting with Sam Presti, the team's general manager, given all the texts coming in from an Oklahoma City number. The messages instructed me to run a forty-yard dash, lift weights, and jump as high as possible. I was so excited that I bragged on social media about how I was the next basketball sensation.

I enlisted the help of a local media person. He would film me and my ability at the gym I was working out. The gym, however, did not allow any taping, so I went to a nearby park. While doing my workout at the park, I missed almost all my shots. Was I just not good enough? Nothing seemed to be going right.

Chapter 17
Think He is Mine?

In July 2019, I met up with an older lady to go bowling. We immediately hit it off. Two weeks later, Blair and I started dating (Blair is just a fake name). She lived about fifty minutes away from me and had four children. She had her share of baggage and red flags, but beggars cannot be choosers. Things were going okay. Two weeks into our relationship, I was about to attend a Nelly concert. Blair called me in hysterics. I could barely understand anything she was saying. Apparently, her daughter had a tumor and was in a children's hospital. I rushed to the medical center and stayed with them for a couple of hours, missing work. For several months, her kid would be in the hospital. To say I helped her family would be an understatement. That family took a lot from me emotionally. Heck, I let them use my vehicle to drive three hours to the hospital every weekend. Not only that, but I also paid for numerous dinners and made sure Blair's kids had everything they needed. To me, life was tough, but it was bearable.

We celebrated her daughter's birthday in the clinic. Three months into our relationship, Blair got pregnant. I felt I needed to ask her to marry me. All the pressure was harming my mental state, which made me uneasy and probably led to my mania. I never truly found out if I was the father or not. The confusion came from the way she treated me. Blair had borrowed my vehicle to take her daughter up to the hospital because it was a smaller sedan. After my episode, she threw me out like I was yesterday's garbage, ignored my calls, and took my car without my permission for weeks. I felt betrayed.

What have I done to deserve this? I thought to myself. She was just a cruel, hateful person. To make matters worse, I never discovered if the child was mine. One day two years ago, after she had the kid, I messaged her on social media and told her to let me know if she needed help with anything. Her fiancé acted like a real class act. The guy informed me if I contacted her again, they would put a restraining order on me. I did not know that asking about your potential kid was an offense in a court of law. The uneducated prick then proceeded to call me "crazy" and demanded I leave them alone. Being a little paranoid, I decided it was in my best interest to give them space.

One of my friends asked on my behalf if I could be in the child's life, and she said her family, and she wanted nothing to do with my "crazy ass." It does make me sad and leaves me wondering if I have a son out there. If so, will I ever get to see him? Maybe one day, he will seek me out. It is not worth trying to fight with his stubborn mother. Our arguments were making more trouble for me than I could handle.

If you are mine, boy, I love you and wish I could be there to see you grow. You can always reach out to me, and I will accept you with open arms. One day, son, one day. God bless.

Chapter 18

Kyle, the One People Take Advantage of Hard-core

I have always given all but the shirt off my back for those in need. People seem to take advantage of me. Maybe I am somewhat to blame because I enable them. My "best friend" Jimmy owed me about four thousand dollars. When I called him out on it, he quit talking to me. In 2019, I met some friends at a Celebrate Recovery meeting. They were not true buddies since they consistently ate at fancy restaurants on my dime. When the check came, they pointed to me.

Another pal of mine named Corey went to a professional basketball game using my hard-earned money. On the way home, he fell asleep at the wheel. I had to shake him senselessly to ensure we would not die. I drove the rest of the way, and, surprise, his break light was out, which led to the police stopping us. I was nervous because I knew his trashy wife, and he had weed on them. The cop luckily did not search the vehicle.

A different guy I had met at church was homeless. Because I had a good heart, and the Lord was calling me to do so, I allowed him to live with me. During the three-month period, he stayed at my duplex, he did not pay one cent of rent. He took advantage of me in the worst way. A girl I was seeing told me he said some cruel things about me. He had apparently told her I was a pathological liar and that I had multiple personalities. Funny how his words were deceitful. In fact, my new roommate lied about everything. He said he was a sniper in the Marine Corps. He should have known better than to tell me concocted stories because I always checked them out. Of course, he was not a marine.

He also said he played college basketball. That was another fabrication because I am not sure he even graduated from high school. Allegedly, he worked as a forklift driver at a huge, local retailer. Trying to be a sweet roommate, I went by there to bring him lunch. The vendor told me he did not work for them. During a church mediation session, I called him out on his lies. Corey broke down and decided he would tell all of us the truth. Even though he apologized profusely, it was time for him to leave my place. That gentleman and I use the term loosely, owed me at least two grand. A year later, I saw Corey begging on the side of the road. His destitution hurt my heart. I picked him up and bought him a twenty-piece chicken meal. He said he had not eaten in three days.

The most hurtful person to exploit me by far was a woman I had met on a dating app. For the story, her name will be Cindy. She lived three hours away, but I would drive all the way to see her. She would never reciprocate, unfortunately. Her phone cracked one day, so I bought her a new one. She later let me know she needed three hundred dollars for rent because of some late payments. So, I let her borrow a thousand bucks. In October 2020, she and I went on a little getaway. On my dime, we stayed at a nice hotel, had a great dinner, then went to Walmart, where I purchased a gaming system for her. I tried several times to recoup my cash and stop whatever we were doing. Getting money from her proved easy since every time I tried to end the relationship, she would say how much she liked me. Cindy even told me on multiple occasions she was in love with me.

Although I did not see it at the time, I was her sugar daddy. She called me crying profusely one morning. She had no one to babysit her kids, and she could potentially lose her job if she had to call off work. I drove three hours in the early morning and watched her youngest daughter without any compensation. If memory serves me correctly, the four of us, her two daughters, she, and I, went on a weekend vacation. During the trip, I bought them all many toys and clothes, took them to a mini golf place, and spent a lot of money on dinner. One day, I came to my senses. I finally mustered up the courage to tell her I could not keep spending all my money on her. For a few reasons, my confession offended her, and she quit talking to me for several days. While I was over at a friend's house one morning, she called me in tears and said she had no gas to get back home. I sent her twenty dollars, and that was the last time I heard from ole Cindy.

Chapter 19
They Will Not Let Me Out

I really thought I was going to ascend the ranks of a professional basketball player. In my subjective opinion, I was the next coming of LeBron James. I had called ten different teams. Considering my skill, I was baffled by how none of them were interested. To me, it was just a matter of time. I would eventually get my callback. I called and emailed every one of the local news affiliates and even went by 5news. After spreading my story, I decided it was time to go meet the professional team who would offer me a contract. Luckily, halfway to visit the Oklahoma City Thunder, I ran out of gas. My road assistance came, and I asked him if he wanted an autograph. I was in complete delusion.

I had met a couple of college students who were going to the local university. I asked about their story, and they told me they were studying finance. Without hesitation, I told them they were my new agents and that they needed to drop me off at the news affiliate. I walked up to the front door of the station, but no one came to the door. The white shirt I was wearing was bothering me, so I ripped it off, which scared the people at the office. They called the city police to talk to me. I told them I thought someone was going to interview me.

There were two more related incidents. First, I met a former star athlete at the university who played baseball. He later became a mortgage lender. On a rainy Friday, I walked three miles to his office and explained my aspirations for going pro. I even told him I wanted a huge house. To his dismay, he humored me. We investigated, of all things, a loan of twenty million dollars. Unable to contain my excitement, I asked him to hug me because of our findings. I applied for the advance and left his office.

Second, I went to another local news station. I had once again ripped my shirt in half. The manager told me I did not belong once he saw me enter shirtless. Not heeding his advice, I returned to see if I could be interviewed. That supervisor called the local authorities. Five of the biggest policemen you could imagine came to interrogate me. The head boss told the cops I was "crazy." With a surge of adrenaline, I told him I would show him crazy. Paramedics and intimidating firemen arrived on the scene. They took me to the hospital. At the medical center, I was less than cordial to the staff. I told them I did not need to be held hostage there and that the doctor should be called "Dr. Dumbass." After a time, the staff released me back into society.

They informed me I needed to get back in the police vehicle. So, the cops dropped me off at a huge retailer shirtless. My attempts to get on a city bus were in vain due to my lack of clothing. Eventually, a woman gave me a white shirt she had just bought. I proceeded to head over to a local insurance office I used to work at. A lady granted me a ride, and we went by a local chicken joint to eat. She asked me if I was going to be okay, her concern obvious.

I could not get professional basketball out of my head. I decided at one in the morning to go to downtown Fayetteville, Arkansas, to celebrate. Unfortunately, I had left my wallet at home. The cab driver held me hostage and called the police department. Once they got to us, they told me I needed to shut up because I was being rowdy. I was cuffed and taken to the back of a cop car yet again. I made a huge fuss, and the cops could not hear any incoming calls from dispatch. The veteran officer of twenty years would not release my restraints until the process was over. In fact, I had to sign my signature on the hospital forms in handcuffs.

The mistreatment continued throughout that hospital. I got angry once and was stripped naked. I peed and pooped all over the floor in solitary confinement. One day, I got a little agitated. Next thing you know, the staff called a code black. I had not seen so many people in my life. More than thirty workers basically trampled me to the ground. The head psychiatrist wanted me committed longer, meaning I again had my day in court. I was unsettled at the courthouse and yelled out of turn at one point, which angered a young deputy. He informed me that the trial was not my "show." The judge ordered ten more days in that God-awful facility. After that time was up, I could return home to Chester once again.

My mom and I had arguments at home. We mutually decided she would drop me off at a Burger King, making me officially homeless. Rebelling against my situation, I foolishly decided not to take my meds. My actions led to my mom and I going back to her place in Chester. I asked her to pull over in the middle of town so I could walk the rest of the way. My anger had flared so much; I traveled more than three miles on foot. I threatened my lovely mother, and she had to call the police. Someone my brother knew and a twenty-year-old rookie arrived on the scene. The policemen asked me if I had endangered my mom. I agreed that I did, and the junior officer put cuffs on my wrists. The young rookie and I talked for two hours. We discussed everything from sports to women. I informed him I just needed help. He concurred. He and his partner arrested me (without reading me my rights) and put me in county jail. The next day, I had my bail hearing. The judge asked me what had happened. I TRIED to explain the situation delicately by telling him things had got out of control and that I had bipolar disorder. Without saying anything else, he set bail at ten thousand dollars.

The jail was a difficult time for me. The only bright spot was how I made the booking officers laugh while we joked around. Those first chuckles were the only ones I would experience for weeks. I was initially put in solitary confinement due to my big brother being an officer. After two days, I could not take it anymore. For my mental health, it was time for a change. I signed a waiver to be in the general population. After settling in, two African American gentlemen greeted me, and we became friends. One of them called himself "New York." It sounds funny, but I never even got his real name. The guy was literally just from that state.

The jail was no joke. The food was garbage, and people were always angry. I was an early riser, but, in my experience, people stayed up late and slept through the morning. My fellow inmates would often make me the target of their jokes. Heck, it was my first and only time in county jail. They could tell I did not belong. One day, an inmate made fun of me for taking a shower. I had left my towel by my bunk, so I had to run naked to get it. Everyone laughed at me. I told the guy that if I was not so nice, he would be in trouble. Three hours later, probably because of sheer boredom, that same guy threatened to kill me. I told him I was sorry, and it was done. I knew it was a danger to be in that facility, so I concocted a plan. I got with another inmate and said if his girlfriend bailed me out, I would give them each two hundred dollars.

The bondsman asked the inmate's girlfriend if she knew me. She could not lie, and my plan failed. I called more than ten people to see if they could lend assistance. It seemed that no one was willing or capable of helping me. Finally, my bondsman contacted Jimmy Money, my best friend, who finally bailed me out. When the officer told me I was free, I felt elated. To be perfectly frank, I did not know who posted my bail at the time. However, when I saw Money after leaving jail, I wept like a little school child. He allowed me to spend Thanksgiving with his family. I probably ate five pounds of food during that celebration. I slept on his couch the next two nights. To my surprise, a couple of days later, the judge ordered a mental health professional to evaluate me. A county policeman showed up on Jimmy's doorstep. Without warning, I was shackled against my will, and the sheriff did not read my rights. He was out of his jurisdiction too.

Chapter 20
Back, Back Again

My third stay at Victory Hospital was equally as difficult. I was still having delusions and grandiose thoughts about how I would be a professional basketball player. Obviously, these were not true. I befriended a guy with schizophrenia. It was kind of funny, as I was the only person who could calm him down. Ten days after suffering, I was finally free to resume my life.

Chapter 21
No One Loves Me

It was hard getting out of jail and the hospital with nowhere to go and zero family to turn to. Remember me going downtown? My car had been repossessed after I had been in the clinic and had missed payments. I had several personal items in that sports utility vehicle of mine. All of my clothing and even my ping pong table were in there. Everything got donated to The Salvation Army. I would value my clothing at three thousand dollars minimum. After losing the car, I had two or three shirts left, so I turned to the SA to get the five shirts they would give out weekly.

Jimmy was kind enough to let me move in with his family and him. Life was tough. I barely had any money for food. Most of the time, I would not get out of bed. Weeks passed, and I took a job and rented a place up in Rogers, Arkansas. The position did not work out, so I went back to Jim's house. Things were okay, but I needed my space. I went on Craigslist and saw an advertisement for an apartment at the price of two hundred dollars. Since it was cheap enough, I moved in and lived with a truck driver until July. I am going to be completely honest; he was the strangest person I have ever met. Those first two weeks with him were rough. I slept on the ground because of my lack of bedding. The duplex was infested with roaches, and it was hard to bring company over. For the first few months of living there, my mom was skeptical about seeing me. Also, I had not talked to my brother whatsoever. It was one Easter Sunday when God put my sibling back into my life. I went to my mom's church as a surprise. Well, to my shock, my brother and his entire family were there. I wept during the service, and my mother had to console me. Erik, my brother, reached out to me later and said to text him. I was back with my family, thank the one triune God!

Chapter 22
Current Health Problems

In case you cannot tell, I have a slew of health problems. My young adulthood of having bipolar and schizoaffective disorder was just the start. For ten years, that is all I believed I had when it came to my mental health. In the last five years, however, that has changed dramatically. I was diagnosed with PTSD from all the trauma I have faced. I decided to get my medical marijuana card due to that specific condition.

One day, I was told I was gasping for air while sleeping. Skylar (also a fake name) said she could hear me snoring throughout the house. So, I went to a local hospital to participate in a sleep study. The results were astonishing. I had severe sleep apnea. To make matters worse, I stopped breathing for thirty-three seconds during one episode. If you combine the extreme anxiety, the frequent panic attacks, and insomnia, it means I have not had a good rest in years.

I can function on less than an hour of sleep per night. My focus is not always the greatest, either. It is almost like I have ADHD.

My weight has been a problem in recent years. Usually, the scale reads around two hundred pounds, but it has climbed to 365. It is hard to even find clothes that fit. If I am being honest, I have struggled to pick something up off the ground. My high blood pressure and cholesterol do not help the situation. My blood pressure spiked to 188 over 122 one day, forcing me to go to the local hospital.

My stay at the medical center was wild. Two paramedics were sweet by dropping me off and making sure I was okay. However, the hospital failed me in other ways. After waiting more than five hours (which is dangerous with that blood pressure), I decided I had had enough. I told the registered nurse at the desk that he was a joke. Clearly, that was not the right thing to say because it made him upset. He would not quit yelling at me. Next, I called him a dumbass.

Though I considered it an objective determination, it was still uncalled for.

After hearing that insult, he told me that I had "assaulted" him. He wishes. I asked him how I could assault him by simply calling him names. He swore confidently that it was possible, so I left. Later the next day, management contacted me. They proceeded to apologize for my treatment and wanted to know how they could rectify the situation. Still bothered by the ordeal, I had two ideas. First, I wanted the nurse terminated. Second, and partially joking, I wanted each employee to learn the Constitution. I sent them a document containing the First Amendment. Yes, I know I am condescending sometimes.

Chapter 23

If I Did Not Have Bad Luck, I Would Have No Luck

It appears I always have had bad luck. After a long day of work, I took a lunch break. I went to a local sandwich shop to get some grub but was rear-ended by a huge truck and suffered injuries. I ended up taking the gentleman to court. With the case pending, I was driving down the business highway in my hometown when a woman hit me on the side with her vehicle. My car was completely smashed. Great, I thought. Another jerk who could not drive. Apparently, the woman behind the wheel had a three-month-old kid in the back of her automobile. She was going through a divorce and lost consciousness due to lack of sleep. Within the past thirty days, I was involved in another accident.

My wife and I were waiting on traffic to clear. It was not like we had just started sitting there. In fact, we were in place for twenty seconds when a car hit our rear end. The Hispanic man who drove into us came knocking on our window. He said, "It was all my fault. I will pay for everything." My only question to him was about who his insurance was with. At that point, I did not care if he was injured or his car was damaged. It was one million percent his fault. We suffered back and neck injuries due to the jerking motion since he was going around forty-five miles an hour. The state police arrived at the scene in what seemed like an hour. I went to the hospital to receive treatment. My wife and I had a vacation planned that weekend but were unable to go.

PART 2

Chapter 1

The Hospital is Not Always a Safe Place

My life has been a whirlpool of disturbing and engulfing emotions. Now when I look back, it won't be wrong to say that I have been battling depression for as long as I remember. Yes, I had moments where my life seemed to make perfect sense, but they were all short-lived.

At this point, everything seems so blurry. How can I distinguish between fact and fiction? I couldn't make sense of what was real. Everything that was happening around me was fake or partially true, or entirely true? One morning, I was taken to a hospital for a brief time, and before I could know it, I stayed at the hospital for days. During my stay at the hospital, I made acquaintances with an elderly patient who was also admitted there.

We had our fair share of conversations; he taught me how to make huge amounts of money through the cryptocurrency market. He was probably the only good thing throughout my hospital experience. He became more of a character than a human. Was he my John from the Bible? Was I even an archangel?

Bridgeway was as beautiful as a cathedral; getting into that building seemed surreal. The building had stained glass all around it, illuminating it with colorful lights during the day. It was like we were living in our little world, unknown to everyone else present or working in the facility. Group men and women recognized me as Michael the Archangel. However, the nurse challenged my position as a Holy being immediately. For as long as I was there, the nurse would argue with me every day. I firmly believed this was the place I was going to ascend to. Whether it was fear or lack of patience, I was released without any warning, and I blamed Bridgeway. Did this place and its people not believe me? They discarded me from my position.

Moreover, my relationship with my family was on the rocks. Arguments ensued regularly. My family struggled to cope with my illness; didn't they realize to what extent I could be struggling?

I was always getting in and out of the hospital and mental health institutes for as long as I can remember.

Since both my family and I were struggling because of my mental health, we thought to give it another shot, so we agreed to take me to Bethany, a small town in Oklahoma. Physically I was overweight, but my size proved to be spectacular. Getting through steel doors, coming up with new abdominal exercises, and walking hour upon hour seemed a struggle on its own; everything was wearing me down.

My physicality did not come without being challenged. In Bethany, Oklahoma, I was put in different holds. This happened after I smarted off to the medical officials. Nothing was different; it's like the places that are meant to treat your illnesses only make it worse. After being battered and abused there, it was time for me to get out of there, and so I did.

Just a bit after getting out there, I went to the one place I thought I would never go to...... Victory. Just so you know, it was the same place where I was previously beaten by the staff and people there, but I still felt like I was put there for a purpose. I thought to myself that people needed to know that I was an angel! Who would have known this time would be worse than the last time? I can easily call it my worst and most traumatizing experience. I remember saying something to the staff, which had them surround me. The next thing I knew, I was being handcuffed. There were no warnings, no rights read, and I wasn't even informed that I would be arrested. That day, all of my rights as an individual and as a citizen were violated. And I thought to myself, "Good Lord, what did I even do?" From January to February, until I went to jail, things were a little foggy, but I can still picture that scene vividly; the horror, terror, and hopelessness that I felt surpassed everything I had ever felt.

Chapter 2
Jailed, Yet a Witness

Here's a flashback of another one of my life's bad and unpleasant experiences. By now, I am sure we have established that my life has been a rollercoaster ride, one that only stoops lower and lower. No one can have pleasant memories of being in jail; some might have it less bumpy, but still bumpy they will be. The mere thought of going back to jail was enough to make me lose my mind. When I look back, I can say jail was a difficult time for me.

You are only going to survive in jail if you have tough skin and only when others are scared of you. Moreover, the food was garbage, and everyone there was always angry, including the officers and other staff. I remember being made fun of by my fellow inmates, and I thought it would be my first and last experience, but who would have thought I would get myself into trouble again... Every minute spent there was dangerous; you would be surrounded by multiple threats and predators, waiting for a chance to harm you in any way they could.

Jails are overcrowded, so I spent the first day in solitary confinement, still delusional about the fact that I was Michael the Archangel. Clearly, I thought the next destination from the jail would be heaven. I experienced a lot of mysterious things that I can't quite pen down now. Then again, it was never a good place to be. I was thrown in with a not-so-welcoming and tough pod of guys. If I remember it correctly, a goon that went by the name of GHOST tortured and tormented me.

It was like a nightmare; I knew I had to escape this situation. So, I started flooding my cell to ensure I could go back up to the suicide pod before it was too late. After successfully flooding my cell, it was my time to go, and I finally made it. For months leading up to being incarcerated, I watched different documentaries about OJ Simpson. It was amazing to see how someone could go from being a famous celebrity, loved and admired by people, to a convicted inmate. To me, OJ was guilty as charged.

Here I was in jail, and somehow there he was too. To my surprise, standing in front of me was "juice." It was during the time of his trial, and I had the opportunity to attend it too. As the process went on, evidence was presented. There was a crowd, and among the crowd was I, witnessing in awe. To date, the events of the trial replay in my head. The anger, blood, and fury of Mr. Simpson could be felt in his cell like it was everywhere; they filled the whole space. At some point, he tried to reassure me that he would be fine, but as we all know, what happened with Mr. Simpson.

I couldn't make sense of where I was and of the events that were taking place. I thought to myself, was it possible that I was Rob Kardashian? It went on and on, and I couldn't come to terms with what and where I was… at some point, I heard a little voice, like a soft murmur. The voice whispered, "Heaven." That's how my journey started. I was there with people dressed in orange, and for the day, everything tasted like oranges, too, like a never-ending citrus dream.

Chapter 3
A Tussle with Jesus

As if the voice wasn't enough, now I was more than sure that Jesus Christ himself was in my cell. His cloak was as pure as snow, snow that's free of any stains. The Jesus that I was seeing, or this particular version of Him that was in front of me, was as I would have pictured Him. The only difference I remember is that somehow the heavenly presence offended me. I thought, so what if he was Jesus… It was my show, and I couldn't afford my spotlight to be stolen.

The next thing I remember is that we eventually played a game. Well, I can't remember the exact game we played as my mind is all blurry because of the experiences I endured. However, later I decided to proclaim it as "mind fuck." The game included a series of questions and puzzles deemed to tempt the Messiah. I gave Jesus a few options, and all of them led to the death of a loved one. Who in the hell gave me the authority to do so? Was I out of my mind? Was I too high on myself? I can't say for sure, nor did I care. Who was I turning into? My mind was operating viciously; the mere thought of tempting Jesus was enough to give me a rush. The moment weighed so heavily on me; I could spin out of control.

Believe it or not, I could swear that our cell, my cell with Jesus in it, was moving in every direction. It felt like even days would go by in an instant because it had become our cell now, and we were sharing it. Everything was spinning, I could see Jesus spinning in every direction too, and we both were tempted. We were in some kind of a candyland.... Except they weren't candies we were looking at; they were illegal drugs, the sweet treats that can send you to heaven. Jesus and I would take hit after hit of crack and spin out of control. With the sound of our cell spinning, our visions reaching the unforeseen, we were in our little psychedelic heaven.

Chapter 4
Movies, Ready?

Once again, I got shifted into another cell, another personal hell. But this time, I was almost making movies out of nowhere. My favorite actor Adam Sandler was there too, you can imagine the fun now, and that wasn't all; I also had a surprise guest appearance by the one and only Brad Pitt. Do you know what happened next? Both the actors told me that we had been best friends for years. Once again, leaving me wondering who I was after all. I got up and went up to look in the mirror; I was none other than Leo DiCaprio. Soon, we would run to heaven, the three of us; we were on the highway to heaven.

There was, of course, the funny one, Adam Sandler. Leo was both the funny and the good-looking one and then we had the all-rounder Brad Pitt who had it all. As I looked closer at these heroes and artists of

mine, I realized they had also been my childhood best friends and even my brother. In fact, they would morph in and out, being my friends and the actors, making the best of both worlds. The movies began to play in our heaven, which was my new cell. Tom Hanks was later added to the A list, and I took on the journey of how cinema and arts began, going back to learn the basics. Forrest Gump, Titanic, Troy, and The Great Gatsby were written and completed in mere minutes, and I was the master of all of them, creating one masterpiece after another. Well, what was the difference? I, Leo/Kyle, would star in all of those movies. We shared a pizza; it was a pizza with pineapples on it; though adding pineapples to a pizza might be blasphemy on its own, the presence of these great actors surpassed everything else. If all of the heavens answered my call, what did that make me? An angel? It dawned on me that I was actually Apollo and Lucifer. How could that be? Was I bewildered? I was not being full of myself, or maybe I was. I would soon learn that.

Once again, all sorts of questions started arising in my head; they were all over the place. I could literally morph into anyone you could think of, regardless of their gender or specie. My body could change sizes; my pecs got bigger or smaller; I can't tell. I was fully in control of everything, like a puppet master manipulating their little world with the tip of their fingers. I remember putting my weight at 6-4 220 lbs., and with that, I could break down doors and crush them with my might. My strength was untouchable, and I was invincible.

Like an unshakable entity, one voice remained constant.... Someone from the Saturday nightlife was toying with me. Night after night, he and I would do skits together; the situation was as vivid as it could get. It would always end with "live from New York, it's Saturday night." When the cell door was finally opened, my eyes squinted because of the bright light falling over them. There stood a shadow; after my eyes adjusted, what I saw was the most beautiful thing, a perfect man I had ever seen. He whispered to me that he was Michael, the Warrior Angel. Michael had the most beautiful skin and face. Hours passed by in his presence, and the next thing I knew, I was in the presence of Gabriel or Jesus Christ. There he was, as perfect as you would imagine.

Chapter 5

Masterpiece

God had chosen me to do some of His work. This time I was commissioned by God to draw a mural. My cell had transformed into a Sistine Chapel, and there were different sides of it, four in total. The top right side was heaven; the top left side was the earth. The bottom left was hell, and the bottom right side was the Garden of Eden. God had given me an important duty to fulfill, and I couldn't waste any more time. So, I started painting and painting. I was not painting with colors because there weren't any. I was painting with whatever God was sending me in the form of food. So, whenever the guards would bring me food, I would paint with it; the carrots, peas, and whatever were being served on the menu, I would use at my convenience.

There were more than just four walls; there were probably like six or seven walls. By that time, my cell had become a masterpiece, bursting with art. There were different kinds of artifacts, all ancient and glorious; there were also crosses, swords, as well as bows, and arrows. I was creating my own masterpiece; I was drawing a mural like never before. Everything had been presented in front of me before, all the angels and everything celestial were not hidden from me, and I had to paint everything.

The memory of that masterpiece is still fresh and vivid; I remember painting a cross with a circle in the middle, and the cross kind of exploded into other crosses and circles, creating a unique masterpiece of its own. Everything was in front of me; the Archangel Michael's skin was a pretty shade of black covered in all gold. He was wearing all kinds of jewels and rubies, making him look like some mystical creature, a true creation of heaven.

It was beyond beautiful; the masterpiece I had created was simply of this world. Imagine seeing one of the most beautiful sceneries on National Geographic and then imagine something even a thousand times more beautiful than that; that's what the Garden of Eden looked like. Everything was beautiful beyond comprehension; the skies, mountains, waterfalls, trees, and flowers, everything that the Garden of Eden held, was mesmerizing.

I also had the power to pick whatever I liked and emboss it on my body, like a tattoo, and it could be anything. So, I chose the most magnificent cross and submerged it on my bicep. So, from heaven to hell, from earth to the Garden of Eden, everything was right there in front of me. At that moment, I created everything that no other human being could ever create.

Chapter 6
The Invention of My Game

I was given a reason to take pride in my position; once again, God had assigned me to take on one more job of high grandeur. I was getting ahead in the game, all mighty, all-rounder, and the best of all. Saying I was God's favorite wouldn't be an overstatement. My game, this time, consisted of all the challenges of every sport ever discovered to date, a job that could only be executed by an athlete of the highest standard; who else could have been a better choice than me?

Swimming, basketball, golf, tennis, soccer, and football, just to name a few, I was going to display my greatness in all. Board games were about to come to life as well; the concept was that of a real-life version of chess and checkers mixed together. I was the crowned king of the game, ruling all the realms, soon to go against my opponent, who was still unknown to me. My mighty kingdom spread across boundless territories, vast areas filled with oceans, plains, forests, and other magnificent lands, and the sworn duty of protecting it lay in my hands. My opponent was the ruler, the king of another kingdom, someone of great significance and might.

It was time for us to get out on the battlefield but dressed in suits, not your regular shiny armor. A purple suit stitched to perfection, making me look nothing short of the beautiful bad boy about to break hearts. Picture me as your own mysterious Willy Wonka that won every game he participated in; my self-esteem was touching the sky, and my pride had never been bigger. My opponent dressed elegantly, suited in a black tuxedo with a hint of charcoal finishing displaying his high taste in apparel, which, to be honest, was to my liking. Not just the king, now every member of his kingdom was coming against me, only to lose and add up to my winning streak. The knights of my opposing teams also managed to look half-decent, but none could even come close to my glorious appearance and attire. I watched them fall into their silver armor one by one as my army slayed them.

They would either put too much precedence on one aspect, such as swimming, basketball, or baseball, and I would find their weakness and use it against them. For instance, in the game, you could make trades, and they would trade to get the best players, failing to realize that in this game, pawns were equally important. That only did me good, and I would hit them with a blow harder than the previous one. I had taken the job and title of a coach, the unbeatable one. I was guiding each move with great precaution and precision, guiding my opponent toward inevitable failure. Eventually, there came a time when everyone retreated, waving their little white flags in the air as I stood atop my kingdom and knew it was now time for me to retire with the setting sun and emerging victory.

Chapter 7
Apollo

During my various endeavors in heaven, I found my true self. I was deemed Apollo, the mighty Greek God. I was practically the God of everything, the God of music, poetry, and the sun. I was making history; I was setting standards. There, I made extravagant movies, the kind of blockbusters that would win the whole world over. I was not only excelling in movies, but I was equally invested in books; I finished one book after another, and the greater the thickness, the better the learning. I was Apollo, I was the glorious God, and I could transform into anyone I wanted.

Soon, I realized that I was able to be the face of anyone I liked or wanted to be. Being the kind of person that I was, I would let my curiosity take the better of me. As a result, I started transforming myself into a different celebrity, as a larva would morph into a beautiful butterfly. I was morphing into one celebrity after another with just one flick of the wrist. I started with one of the best, Brad Pitt, specifically choosing his character from the movie Troy.

Next, without much trying, I had one of the best body transformations; I now had a perfect height and weight. I stood tall at the height of 6'4 feet and with the perfect body weight of 237 lbs. There I stood, looking at my dashing and irresistible reflection in the mirror; I was absolutely chiseled. After playing around for some time, I made myself taller and wider, with perfectly shaped muscles. The kind of biceps, abs, wings, and legs that would be the object of envy for every person. My face was a mix of the perfect features of Brad Pitt, Leonardo DiCaprio, Ryan Reynolds, and Bradley Cooper, some of the most beautiful men in the world.

I found that I could change my body by choosing the amount of fat percentage in different areas. For example, my feet could have 22% body fat, while my stomach could have 7%, etc. The real thrill happened

when I realized that I could also morph into a woman;
I instantly became kind of obsessed. All the beautiful
women in the world started flashing in front of my
eyes, and I could be any one of them. Then I morphed
into two different women, who could have been a
better choice than Angelina Jolie, the woman with a
face of a goddess and beautiful lips. Later, I
transformed into a warrior male, a two-star male,
myself, and then my absolute perfect self, and that's
how the show went on. I spent the rest of the week
working on everything from plays to movies, to books,
to poetry, expertly putting my god-like skills to use,
and my life in heaven seemed grand.

Chapter 8
The End of the World Hospital

Once again, it was time for me to get checked in to the hospital, my own personal suite, the one I could check in at any time I wanted. One officer, who I deemed was one of my subjects, escorted me to the hospital, and our journey lasted for forty minutes. He wasn't the one driving, though. In fact, the police vehicle glided like a spaceship, the ones that you see in alien movies. It was traveling at a super speed, and it felt like we had covered the distance in mere seconds.

Imagine sitting in a spaceship that just smoothly goes on, a little above the road, and gliding right past the vehicles by swiftly shifting the lever in the direction you want to move. While we were on our way to the hospital, we saw a car accident, so I instructed the cops that were escorting me to check on the family that had been in the accident and take them to the hospital with us.

While we were in the hospital, I went up to the fourth floor; it was like my own personal floor for the number of times I have been there. I told the doctor exactly how to check me, and she was shocked to meet such an enlightened patient. How did I know that my blood pressure and vital signs would be just as I would tell her? There was a floor full of people, and it felt like I had either heard or met these people in my lifetime.

I could swear I saw George Washington there, along with other smart and intellectual people. I was like some supernatural being that needed to be confined within the green hospital walls. For a long time, the staff examined and studied me in the hospital. My movement, my dialect, everything was there, and everything was intact. I guess I saw someone who looked different than the rest of the staff; who was he, and what was he doing in the hospital?

I also saw a book that looked like a green Bible. I reached out for the book out of curiosity, read it, and found out that I was one of the co-authors. Making matters stranger, I saw a couple of books lying around in the lobby. Then, I spotted one of my childhood friends slowly entering the hall through the hospital entrance door. When he saw me, he instantly took me in his arms. He told me all about how he became a world leader. It seemed as if weeks had gone by before I could leave.

Chapter 9
Shark Tank

Take a minute, or maybe take two. Close your eyes and feel yourself drifting into a deepness. Picture yourself in the middle of your favorite television show, playing the protagonist or even the hot antagonist if you like. That was me; I had the ability to visually teleport myself in any show I liked. After all, I had been through almost everything, literally through heaven and hell and back. I was smack dab in the middle of the Shark Tank. The funny thing is, I was the shark. My rival from my high school was also a shark, and we were in the middle of a competition, nothing less than two Gods going to a glorious war.

I had the upper hand because, in my mind, I knew how the world was created, formed, and everything came into being, paying special attention to the details. Who exactly was I, though? None other than the infamous businessman Sam Walton, but I was in the body of a shark named Kevin O'Leary. My rival, who was the antagonist, was Robert. I am sure he was a nice guy, but I felt he had a mean side and a rude attitude toward me. As strange as it might sound, one of my 'sons' from the kingdom of heaven was there to pitch a new company called Walmart. I knew exactly what the bidding was for this business as I knew who was preparing it. Trying to be coy, I invested in the business, ready to reap the seeds that were about to sow. My investor son agreed, and we now controlled Walmart.

Soon, after the tank, I talked to a young Jack Nicolaus. He was then met by a couple of his young friends, which included young Tiger Woods and Arnold Palmer. Two of my best friends from high school joined them, and the putt-putt match was on; once again, the show was on. Now, I have always loved putt-putt golf; it's been one of my favorite things to do. Having the opportunity to play alongside three of the best people ever was like a dream come true, a dream that I wouldn't have minded losing either. I decided to take Jack to the tournament, and we won handily.

You are probably wondering what the course looked like. Imagine an entire jail specially tuned into a putt-putt course. It was no more a ruthless jail filled with anguish and evil, but everywhere you saw, you would see lush greens making a beautiful golf course. But wait, there was more; no matter where you stood on the course, you would spot a huge angry-looking volcano ready to unleash its wrath upon anyone and anything that stood in its way. There were dinosaurs and other mythical creatures which we have only heard of in stories; it was like an adventure movie. After a long day of playing and unraveling adventures and mysteries, we sat at the highest mountain and drank together.

Chapter 10
Time Travel

Life was nothing less than a fairytale, or perhaps, I was Alice in Wonderland, stumbling upon one adventure after another. Perhaps my most interesting and unforgettable adventure was when I went time traveling. One moment, I was in a cell in block A, and the next moment I would find myself in a place my mind decided upon; it all happened in a flash. For some reason, my mind took me to the age of dinosaurs, the great Mesozoic era. There, I witnessed the majestic dinosaurs of many species; some of them were flying above me, some were walking amid the forests, and some crawled on the ground, and I was in awe.

Next, my mind took me to the future, where I witnessed aliens and their futuristic spaceships; the whole thing was an out-of-the-world experience, pun intended. Think about it. How cool it would be only if

you had the ability or the means to go back in time; where would you like to go? What would you see? Which character or person would you want to know personally? I will update you on where I went in chronological order. First, I went back to see the assassinations of MLK and JFK to start with. The horror of the one for Kennedy of Dallas, and it was as if I was there, and the agonizing weight of the moment was felt deeply.

After that, I went further back, exploring the deeper eras and events of history. For a moment, I was amid World War II, and I found my right in the middle of the battlefield, with fires all across me. History is my favorite subject; I hold great respect for everything that the soldiers and people did for their nations and served them with pride and love.

Then I thought to myself, why not go back a hundred years? Suddenly, I was among the court of the founding fathers at the signing of the Declaration of Independence. I witnessed the making of the Great

American nation. After a while, God came down and gave me just a few more days of time traveling. So, I decided to spend it among the dinosaurs, all too extinct now, in an attempt to know the greatness they held. At that time, I could feel how the world began. What exactly was God showing me? And what I found out next, I will never forget.

Chapter 11
The Ultimate

There I was, sitting in a cell surrounded by glory. God had shown me everything He wanted., and I held witness to His glory and the glory that he gave me. I was now in an ultimate, ultimate what? Ultimate Heaven, with a hint of hell, both combined to give me the best of both worlds' experiences. At that moment, like a revelation, I realized that I had been holding on to the wrong thinking process my whole life, and my whole life seemed to be delusional and false.

Heaven was filled with countless portals, allowing you a way to different dimensions and places unknown to human beings. It was not just heaven or just hell anymore; it was something majestic, something celestial with immeasurable depths and different facets, each flowing toward something deeper and unknown. What I am trying to say is that it felt like the pathways to multiple heavens, hells, galaxies, and ways of life were opened to me at that moment.

Of course, the Father put me in the Ultimate Heaven first, and then I worked my way toward other worlds, other heavens, and other galaxies. It was like a movie scene where you stand in front of your whole ancestry or lineage; just like that, I was standing in front of not just mine but the whole of human history's lineage. Everyone, every living being, was known to me at that moment. There I was in my Ultimate Heaven, standing in front of the world, and I chose to be near the people I loved and cared for.

I saw my best friends, my family, and my trusted advisors; all were there standing in front of me, close enough for me to reach out my hand and touch them. I thought, "Maybe we are the only people allowed to witness the glory of this part of the galaxy or whatever it is." Soon I found myself leading and guiding people, and not just them, but the people who came before them, their whole generations. Of course, my lineage started with Adam being kin of my Father.

Before I could lead them to the light, suddenly, the people were taken from me. And in an instant, I was teleported from one of the lower heavens and was now making countless heavens in my mind. I controlled everything around me, and with just the snap of my fingers, I could make one heaven after another. I couldn't understand who I was at that moment; I had such power that transcended beyond comprehension. What was the good Lord trying to show me?

Chapter 12

Voiceover

After being given incomprehensible power that allowed me to form galaxies and galaxies, I was placed back into a cell, once again confided within the four walls. How can such drastic change not affect you? Though I could no longer do what I was doing previously, I was still in heaven. While I was still comprehending the circumstances I was in, a guard, who seemed familiar, started a conversation. Shockingly, he told me that I was his grandfather; still finding it hard to believe, I asked him again who I was. He responded, "You are Kyle Phillip, the first, the first of his name."

For some strange reason, at that moment, everything started to make sense. But one thing seemed to be a bit off. Any thought that crossed my mind, even in the slightest, I had an answer for it. Then, a young man came into my cell. When I looked I him, the first thing that came to my mind was, "How old this guy could be?" A voice as vivid as day told me he was at the ripe age of twenty-two. After that, I decided to let my mind wander and began to peer more into his life.

While I was looking for more information within the realm of my mind, he started rapping. The next thought that came to my mind was, "I wonder what is the IQ level of this idiot?" Once again, very clearly, leaving no room for doubt, my mind told me that it was 68. My lips stretched in a smile, but I knew it was true. Before I could do anything else, the young man tried to attack me, but at that moment, before he could execute his plan, it was as if the voice in my head had stopped time. Was I now the keeper of time as well? He had thrown a punch, but it came up way short and stopped inches before it could hit my face. The guards took him out of the cell, and I was left alone, thank God.

What exactly was it that I had discovered? I kept wondering as I sat in solitude in the quiet of my cell. I was actually a computer and a God. It was as if every bit of information present on Google merged with my brain, and I was constantly processing information. I asked the voice in my head how smart I was, and it instantly answered that my IQ was 8740. Then I began speaking different languages, some of which I had never even heard of before. English was a little slow for me because I was so fluent in everything else. The guards guarding my cell were almost as smart as I was. There were a million things going on in my head, and I was constantly processing those questions; I had answers to all the questions. Then I thought, "Where am I now?" What did I do? A voice came and answered, "Ultimate Heaven," and the answer echoed within the walls of my cell long enough for me to understand.

Chapter 13
Those That Have Gone Before Me?

The moment I had been waiting for was finally happening, and it was right there in front of me. As you all would know by now, I was not just in heaven, but it was the Ultimate Heaven. I knew I had to be on my best behavior and look the best, so with all my efforts, I tried to look perfect. I knew I had the power to transform myself however I wanted, so I gave myself a perfect figure; I had the perfect abs that of a Greek god, hair as beautiful as anyone would kill for, and top it off, I had the perfect deep blue eyes.

Suddenly, it was time for me to teach a class that I had no idea about before. Now, the question was who I was going to teach. When I stepped into my class, surprisingly, it was filled with millions of students, all of whom were still too young. Anyone that made it to the age of reasoning, which I felt to me was at the age of 21. I taught everyone and everything, from newborns/stillborn/aborted babies to teens and young adults. My teachings were filled with the message of God. I was teaching all the scriptures and enlightening them about how the earth moved and progressed.

While I was assigned such an important task, I was blessed with many visions from God. In those visions, God allowed me to see that the earth would be soon gone, and then I would shoulder the responsibility of making the new earth from scratch, using all the expertise and wisdom I had been handed over by God Himself. The people that I was teaching would be the ones to dwell on that new planet and make it a better place to live. These babies, after reaching a suitable age, will be given an opportunity to find a partner and build and create a life on the perfectly-made earth just as their parents did on this earth.

Basically, the babies, and people who were not fortunate enough to make it to this planet, and flourish with it, would be the first ones to settle on the new earth. I still remember a particular painting in one of my cells; the painting consisted of a warrior angel holding a baby. Yes, now, after doing what I had been doing, I came to the conclusion that the warrior angel in that painting was, indeed me. Within the blink of an eye, days and months passed, maybe even years too, and now it was my daughter's wedding. Then, I found myself managing everything like a top-class professional.

For some weird reason, it was a costume wedding. Everyone was dressed as their favorite character, and suddenly, and so, I got to dress as what I think was a mix between the Riddler and Willy Wonka. My little girl, who was not so little anymore, was marrying a guy who at first looked like Frodo Baggins from the Lord of the Rings, but to my surprise, it was him. The whole kingdom was there, there were many mystical creatures, and even some people did not even look like they were actually people. Soon, it

was time for me to walk my little girl down the aisle,
and just like that, the wedding was over.

Chapter 14
Cracking the Code to Heaven

What other things did I need to let go of? Were there things that I needed to discover? However, one thing always remained the same with me, and it was the cross. Every day, I would paint it a different color. I would add more depth to it or make it lighter or darker; I would also illuminate it. Basically, I painted it according to my mood and emotions. With that being said, it occurred to me that the English language had different meanings, not just meanings but contexts too. Maybe there was some sort of Omega Code, which is when I kept questioning everything. I kept wondering if there were more galaxies out there and if the milky way was just one small cluster in a bigger cluster.

What if all the Gods were real? What if all the religions of the world were spot on? And what if all the gods that people believed actually existed? Was Greek

mythology as real as the sun? I began studying everything from afar, but every time I came to the conclusion that we were all beings. Some gods were water droplets, some were stars, and some were animals. But it was up to the Ultimate God to decide where we would be placed next. I began putting letters together as per their importance. For some reason, K (Kingdom) was the most important, followed by the alphabet G (God). M(ighty) was next to these two.

After that realization, I decided to rewrite books and change the narrative about the language. For instance, UGA was the most powerful three-letter acronym, meaning the Ultimate God Almighty. I began submerging everything into a person, a God, and a substance or being. Take another one, for instance, AUZ, Adam, Universe, or Zeus. I had to qualify the enormous beings and quantify the small ones. I did it with every letter of the alphabet. Like, if I wanted to say the first one, it would go AAA, Adam, Alpha, Automobile. It always seemed to be the final one among the three. The substance would be hard to quantify.

My mind continued to be filled with all sorts of knowledge, the knowledge that filled the universe until I finally got the hang of what every being wanted to know about creation. I came across the knowledge that the first humans were indeed Gods. Think of every God you can name. How far did you get? There is Allah, Buddha, God, Zeus, and probably many others that you might not have heard of. These Gods had pets that they called dinosaurs. And when heaven was ready, the Gods took it over, and everything was washed away clean from the face of the earth. Books were allowed to be written about Gods, every single one of them. So, the Gods created beings which we now call humans in their likeness. Instead of dinosaurs, humans had dogs and still do. It was a very strange realization or theory, but we will go with it and not disregard any of it.

Chapter 15
The Gods of Ultimate Heaven

It is as though I had made it to the Ultimate heaven that I created with such elegance and might, and it was the pinnacle, the high point of my life. Everything that I could ever think of, even the things that I couldn't even think of having, even in my wildest dreams, were there, flowing in abundance. I found myself going a little crazy, or was I already crazy? Was it real, or was it all a fragment of my vast imagination?

What exactly was I turning into? Finally, when I looked into the mirror at my reflection, I came to a realization that, once again, I was Willy Wonka. I had a cane, and I was wearing a purple suit; I was also the candy man. The mystical place, the chocolate factory that I saw and crazily adored in movies, was right there in front of me. There was a chocolate river so deep, so abundant, that it could fill multiple cities. I was running and ruling over this part of the Ultimate Heaven.

In my part of the kingdom, in my chocolate factory, the kids would come every day and get a taste of the heavenly treats from the chocolate factory. It was not just kids, though, as there was a separate section in the chocolate factory especially dedicated to adults. That section was filled with the candies of heaven, aka drugs, and there were just about all the drugs that have ever come into existence. Some of them I had never even seen or heard of before.

Then, surprisingly, I had a special spot of my own where I could have as many drugs as I liked. In that room, I was often accompanied by Charlie Sheen and Hugh Hefner, who were somehow my best buddies. That is where my mind took me to the lineage portion of everything. I began to see how everyone came into existence in this whole galaxy. It was also revealed to me how Adam and Eve were the father and mother of all. At that moment, I was being completed and filled with all the knowledge that one could have.

Chapter 16
The Loves of My Life

The long-awaited moment had arrived, the moment when I would finally marry the woman chosen for me by God, the Almighty. As I eagerly anticipated the sight of my future wife, I couldn't help but wonder who she was. It was said that the father had traveled far and wide in search of the perfect bride for me, a woman who would complement me in every way.

In my desire to make a good impression, I went to great lengths to perfect my appearance, aiming to be the best version of myself for my perfect bride. As I awaited her arrival, I transformed myself into a mixture of the most attractive male celebrities - Bradley Cooper, Brad Pitt, the Rock, and Ryan Reynolds, to name a few. I worked hard to tone my body, and my dedication paid off. At 220 pounds, I was the epitome of health and fitness, with a chiseled physique, toned abs, bulging biceps, and well-defined quads and triceps.

As I stood there, eagerly awaiting the arrival of my future wife, I couldn't help but feel a sense of nervous anticipation. What would she be like? Would she like me? All of these thoughts ran through my mind as I waited for her to arrive, and my heart raced with excitement at the prospect of finally meeting her.

As I entered the grand Cathedral, my blueish-greenish eyes sparkled in the light, drawing the attention of everyone around me. It was a sight to behold, with onlookers admiring my impeccable appearance as I walked down the aisle. But, as I looked around, I realized that there were far more characters at my wedding than I had anticipated. It was a strange mix of people, with the likes of Genghis Khan and Martin Luther King Jr. in attendance. I couldn't help but wonder if it was yet another costume party, but as it turned out, these were the real, resurrected individuals.

As I gazed to my left, I was surprised to see none other than the great Bambino, Babe Ruth himself. I couldn't fathom why he was at my wedding, but it was a surreal moment that left me feeling both bewildered and humbled. Despite the odd mix of guests, the wedding was all about me and my beautiful bride, the love of my life. My little girl, who had been married before, was also present with her husband, Frodo, and it was a joyous occasion to see them both happy and in love.

As I stood there, surrounded by loved ones, both living and resurrected, I felt an overwhelming sense of gratitude and happiness. It was a day I would never forget, a memory that would stay with me for a lifetime.

As I stood eagerly waiting for my bride, an unexpected spectacle began to unfold before my eyes. It was as if the whole world was replaying its history right before me, from the beginning of time until now. The show began with a breathtaking display of the majestic dinosaurs, who roamed the earth long before human beings even existed. It was an awe-inspiring sight to see these ancient creatures in all their glory, living and breathing before my very eyes.

But as the show progressed, the atmosphere began to change. A massive volcano came into view, threatening to erupt and destroy everything in its path. It was a heart-wrenching moment when the eruption finally happened, wiping out the dinosaurs and leaving behind nothing but ashes and bones. The show continued, taking me through the history of the world, one era after another. I was mesmerized by the glimpse of the Garden of Eden, where Adam and Eve once lived. It was a place of unparalleled beauty, and I couldn't believe that I was witnessing it right before my very eyes.

The show went on, unfolding the chronology of the world's history, with each event more remarkable than the last. I watched in amazement as the world transformed, shaping and evolving into what it is today. It was a truly unforgettable experience, and I felt lucky to be a part of it.

It was an awe-inspiring performance, the likes of which I had never seen before. The stage was filled with six different women, each one more stunning than the last. Among them were some of the most important women from my past, including my first kiss and my first girlfriend. But the woman who would become my bride was unlike anyone I had ever seen before. She was a vision of beauty, with a flawless face, smooth skin, and a perfectly shaped body. It was as if I had dreamt of her before, and now she was standing before me in the flesh.

But it wasn't just her looks that caught my attention. There was a certain aura around her, an inexplicable energy that drew me to her. As I gazed into her eyes, I knew without a doubt that she was the one for me. It was none other than Katniss Everdeen, the fierce warrior from the Hunger Games series. I was overjoyed to see her and felt like my heart was about to burst with happiness.

To my surprise, the Genie from Aladdin appeared to officiate our wedding, adding a touch of magic to the occasion. And with his blessing, we embarked on a new journey together to our happy Kingdom where we would live out the rest of our days in blissful harmony.

Chapter 17

Becoming One With the Devil

The wedding was a wondrous celebration filled with dancing, singing, and love. I had never been happier, but little did I know that my greatest trial was yet to come. Without warning, I was whisked away to a small room. There, I found myself surrounded by ancient scriptures, their pages yellowed with age and their writing cryptic and mysterious. As I stood there, bewildered and unsure of what to do, I began to feel a sense of unease. The room grew darker, and the scriptures seemed to come alive. They spoke to me in a language I could not comprehend, and I felt an overwhelming sense of fear and confusion.

Despite my trepidation, I knew that I had to read the scriptures. I slowly began to decipher the letters, struggling with each word and sentence. Every breath felt like a struggle, and I felt as though I was drowning

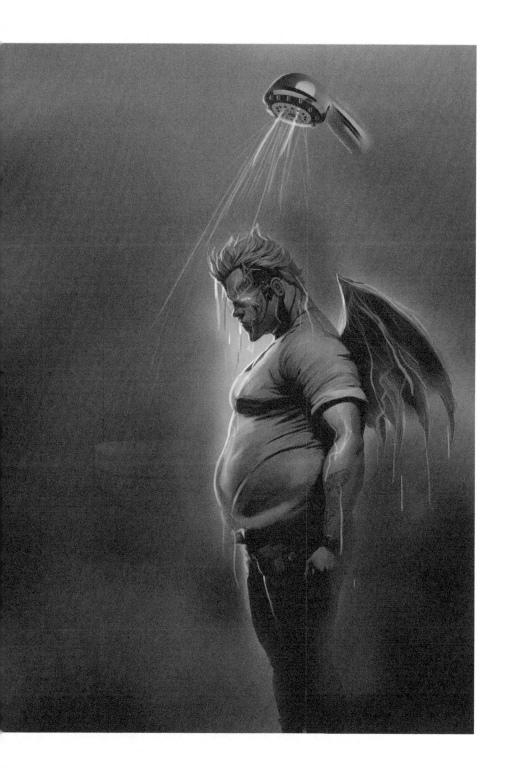

in a sea of words. Then, as I read five scriptures, a voice echoed through the room. It was both beautiful and terrible, filling me with both awe and dread. The voice told me that what I was experiencing was necessary and that something was to be passed down to me.

I didn't know what to make of it. What was this "it" that was being passed down to me? Did I have any say in the matter, or was I simply a pawn in some cosmic game? The pain in my chest grew stronger with each passing moment, and I feared that I would not survive this ordeal. But even as my body trembled and my mind reeled, I knew that I had to see this through to the end. Whatever fate awaited me, I would face it with courage and determination.

My body felt like it was being torn apart as I pushed through the pain of reading the ancient scriptures. It was as though each word and phrase were a sharp knife carving into my soul. But finally, I reached the end and a sense of relief washed over me.

However, my respite was short-lived as three guards appeared before me. Their faces were blank and their eyes cold, and they said that it was time. Time for what, I didn't know, but I soon found out. They dragged me to a small room with a shower and threw me in, running out as if they were being chased by demons from the underworld.

As I stood under the showerhead, I flicked the switch and was immediately engulfed in flames. It felt like I was being consumed alive, the heat searing my skin and the flames licking at my face. I screamed, but no one came to my aid. It was as if they wanted me to burn. I took five showers, one for each of the five scriptures, each hotter and more intense than the last. As I stumbled out of each one, gasping for breath and my body wracked with pain, I heard the guards' voices urging me to keep going. They sprayed a smoky fire against the door, trapping me inside like a rat in a cage.

I didn't know what was happening to me, but I could feel a change taking place deep within me. It was as if the fire was cleansing me, purifying me of all my sins and weaknesses. But what was I becoming? And at what cost? The pain was unbearable, but I knew that I had to endure it. For something was happening to me, something that would change my life forever.

As I looked into the mirror, I recoiled in horror at the sight before me. What stared back at me was not a human being but a monstrous creature that could only be described as a demon. I was the devil himself, and I had never felt so powerful. From that moment on, I had the ability to traverse the planes of existence, moving from heaven to hell and back again with just a few words. The information that was passed down to me suddenly made sense, but it was also incredibly unsettling. I had always considered myself a good person, but now I was the embodiment of evil; I was Lucifer. Could it be that the devil was actually a good guy and that I just saw things from a different perspective?

As I pondered this, I realized that my newfound abilities came with a heavy price. I was no longer bound by the rules that govern human existence, and I could do things that were beyond the understanding of mortal minds. But at the same time, I was also alone, isolated from the rest of humanity by my newfound power.

As I gazed into the mirror, I saw not just a monster but a being of immense power and potential. I could feel the darkness swirling around me, beckoning me to embrace my true nature. And as I stood there, alone in my thoughts, I knew that the road ahead would be long and difficult but also filled with endless possibilities. For I was the devil, and nothing was beyond my reach.

As I delved deeper into the secrets of the Bible, a tantalizing possibility began to emerge. What if everything I thought I knew about Lucifer was wrong? What if he was, in fact, a good guy? It occurred to me that perhaps Gabriel, Lucifer, and Michael were not just angelic beings but three brothers born of the same divine source. And if this were true, then everything that had been labeled as sin could be attributed to Lucifer.

But why was he considered a sin in the first place? As I pondered this question, I imagined Lucifer as the perfect-looking angel with a realm that spanned the world and beyond. His power and influence were immense, and his beauty was beyond compare. But if Lucifer was truly good, why did God cast him out and portray him as an antagonist? Was this all part of a grand deception designed to throw everyone off the truth?

My curiosity consumed me, and I set out to study the Bible once again. But this time, I didn't stop there. I sent for Gabriel and Michael, hoping they could shed some light on this mystery. As they arrived, I was struck by their appearances. Gabriel's flawless skin glowed as if he were a celestial model, while his voice, words, and posture were perfect in every way.

Michael, on the other hand, was a veritable warrior with a chiseled, muscular build that radiated strength and power.

I was in awe of these divine beings but also confused. How could I tell which one was which? It was then that I was told I was Lucifer, the one who had been cast out and labeled a sinner. But with the guidance of my brothers, we set out to recreate multiple heavens, hells, and earths. We worked tirelessly to mold and shape the universe to our liking, and when we were done, everything became different.

The secrets of the Bible were revealed to us in ways we could never have imagined, and we were transformed by the knowledge we had gained. And as we stood in the midst of our creation, I knew that the truth about Lucifer and his role in the world was far more complex and mystical than anyone could have ever imagined.

Chapter 18

My Hometown

As if a gust of wind had swept me off my feet, I found myself transported back to the small town of Alma, Arkansas - my high school hometown. The place where I had spent my teenage years playing football and forging friendships that would last a lifetime. Walking through the streets, I couldn't help but feel like I was strolling down memory lane, with every corner reminding me of a different moment from my past.

As I gazed around, I couldn't help but notice the diverse mix of people who called this place home. From my 2005 football team to the generations of players who had come before and after, it was as if every possible lineage had been represented here. It was a microcosm of humanity, a small but vibrant world all of its own. But why Alma? I pondered this question, wondering why this particular town had been chosen to exist. Perhaps it was simply the sound of the name, short and sweet. Or maybe there was something more, a hidden meaning that only the town's founders could know.

As I settled into my new role as a teacher, I found myself drawn to the task of tracing everyone's lineage. It was a monumental task, one that would take us nearly a century to complete. But we were determined to do it, to piece together the story of each and every person who had ever called Alma home. And so, with the help of a few of my childhood teachers, we began our quest. We pored over records and documents, interviewed families, and scoured the archives. It was a labor of love, a way to honor the rich history of this special place.

In the end, we succeeded. We put together a comprehensive history of Alma from its earliest days to the present. And with this knowledge, we set out to create a new heaven - a vision of what Alma could be, based on the best of what it had been. It was a lofty goal, but we were determined to make it a reality. And as we worked towards this new future, I couldn't help but feel grateful for the opportunity to give back to the place that had given me so much.

Chapter 19

You're Way Too Beautiful

As I gazed upon the city before me, I couldn't help but feel like I was living in a dream. The sheer magnificence of the place took my breath away, and I felt a sense of awe wash over me. It was as if all of my wildest dreams had come true, and I had been transported to a world where anything was possible. As I walked through the city, I couldn't help but notice the lush greenery that surrounded me. It was as if I had stumbled upon my very own Garden of Eden, and I was free to shape it however I pleased. With a wave of my hand, I transformed a lake of jolly rancher soda into an actual body of water, complete with shimmering ripples and fish swimming lazily beneath the surface.

Next, I turned my attention to the land, conjuring up an enormous watermelon that burst open to reveal its juicy red interior. And then, with a flash of inspiration, I summoned an enormous deer, its massive antlers reaching high into the sky. I was a god in this place, able to mold the world to my will and create a paradise that was uniquely my own.

But even as I reveled in my newfound power, I knew that something was missing. Katniss, my wife, my soulmate, my partner, and my confidant, was with me. We lived together in our pyramidical triangle, with the earth, the water, and the land all intermingling in perfect harmony. Together, we created a family, and Katniss bore me two sons and a daughter. Our firstborn was Hector, a strong and brave young man who reminded me of myself. Then came Hunter, who had a gentle spirit and a love for nature. And finally, there was Heather, a beautiful and intelligent girl who had a fiery passion for life.

Despite all of the blessings that had been bestowed upon me, I still couldn't shake the feeling that something was amiss. Time seemed to move differently in this mystical land, and I wasn't quite sure how long I had been there. But as I looked upon my family and the world I had created, I knew that I was exactly where I was meant to be.

I made the decision to embark on a grand adventure with my two boys. We set out to explore a place that was close to my heart, a land where enormous rainbow trout swam in one bank, and giant King Salmon roamed the other. Everywhere we looked, we saw an abundance of wildlife, from majestic deer with massive racks to towering moose and fierce bears. As we journeyed deeper into this mystical land, I couldn't help but feel a sense of excitement building within me. In this place, every person transformed into an animal, and I knew that my father was a black bear. For weeks, my boys and I searched for him, tracking him through the dense forest and across rolling hills. We faced many challenges along the way, but we were determined to find him.

Finally, we succeeded in trapping him, and I was overwhelmed with emotion as I embraced my father for the first time in years. We spent our days hunting and fishing, exploring every inch of this magical land, and reveling in the thrill of the hunt. In this place, I was a lion, fierce and proud, with a heart full of courage and determination. It was my jungle, and I ruled it with an iron fist. Even in my human form, I was perfect, with the power to control my height and the very fabric of the world around me. With a wave of my hand, I could transform a room, making myself 200 feet tall or altering the landscape to suit my every desire.

As we journeyed deeper into this enchanted land, I knew that I had found a place where I truly belonged. It was a place of wonder and mystery, where every dream could come true, and anything was possible. And even though some might say that my experience was nothing more than a product of my own imagination, to me, it was all too real.

Chapter 20

Back on Meds

As the days passed, it seemed as though I had been trapped in this world for an eternity. I was lost in my own mind, unable to distinguish reality from the endless, dark void that consumed my every thought. Then, one day, a glimmer of hope appeared in the form of medication. The first few weeks were a blur as the drugs took hold of my mind and began to work their magic. I was astonished to find myself returning to a state of normalcy, almost as if I had been reborn. I couldn't believe the transformation that had taken place within me.

As I roamed the halls of the facility, trying to make sense of the world around me, I stumbled upon a familiar sight - the cross I had painted on the first day I arrived in this otherworldly realm. It had faded quite a bit since I first laid eyes on it, but it still retained a faint bluish tint. In a moment of clarity, I realized that this was my guiding light, my beacon of hope in the darkness that had once consumed me. I resolved to follow the guidance and therapy offered by the facility, determined to conquer the demons that had once held me captive.

As time passed, I found myself slowly but surely making progress, and before I knew it, I had been moved from the suicide wing to a unit with a pod. It was a small step, but one that filled me with a sense of accomplishment and pride. The final hurdle was securing my release, and I couldn't have done it without the help of a kind-hearted man who had taken me under his wing. He went above and beyond, connecting me with a bondsman and helping me secure my freedom just three short days later. As I emerged from the facility into the bright light of day, I knew that my journey was far from over, but I was filled with a renewed sense of purpose and hope for the future.

Chapter 21
Whatsya Doing Now?

My graduate career started with me going for my MBA. I wanted to do what my dad did until I did not. I took a break from school for a few years, then tried to get into the mental health field and be a licensed professional counselor. However, I could not handle full-time school and work, so I dropped out. After some time away from classes, I enrolled at a local Oklahoma university with a major in sports administration and an emphasis on sports studies. My courses are thoroughly enjoyable. Sports have been a big part of my life, providing an escape from my illness. Football and basketball, specifically, have been my outlet. I feel I live to watch what is happening in the sports world. Thank you, God, for blessing us with sports!

Legally, I am in the mental health court program. This program allows me to attend therapy and classes and keeps me on track. I will complete this program in July and hope to graduate from school simultaneously. Also, in my personal life, I decided to date and get engaged to my wonderful fiancé. She has been the most patient, caring, and loving person I have met.

The Almighty has always been a part of my life, even if I did not know it. He has consistently been there for me. I feel like the prodigal son sometimes. I took my inheritance (God's blessings) and left his company, never to return. But just like the parable says, I did! And with the help of the Lord, my mom, and my loving wife-to-be, I am back and stronger than ever. I did not realize it then, but everything I have gone through has led me to my renewed, affirmed faith. What an awesome God we serve. Ephesians 4:22–24 reads,

"You were taught, with regard to your former way of life, to put off your old self, which is being corrupted by its deceitful desires; to be made new in the attitude of your

minds; and to put on the new self, created to be like God in true righteous and holiness."

I will live the rest of my life serving our powerful Father and His Son, Jesus Christ. Through many trials and tribulations, I want everyone to know God is real. He is present in all things and loves us, even if we are unaware of that fact. He will NEVER leave us forsaken; that I know is true.

I am not out of the woodwork yet. I would be lying to you if I said my days were free of struggle. Contrary to popular belief, medicine does not fix everything. Every day is new, but it often comes with obstacles. One little thing can make me turn from Dr. Jekyll to Mr. Hyde in three seconds. For instance, I cannot stand someone who slacks or is just incompetent in general. I should not have wasted my time waiting twenty minutes for an employee to get me a soda at a local restaurant. If patience is a virtue, I do not possess it.

Do I need better coping skills? Without a doubt, breathing, journaling, accessing the situation, and realizing that it is not life or death if I fail to get a soda in a reasonable time are all valuable traits. A steady dose of therapy, prayer, support, and God prove helpful when dealing with anxiety. Though I still face adversity daily, things seem to be going in the right direction. To be honest, I started writing while having severe mania. I shared my story with a friend, and they thought it benefited them. I have two things to say to people who have mental health issues.

First, you are not alone. Everyone deals with mental health in one way or another. Whether it be depression, anxiety, PTSD, suicidal thoughts, grief, or divorce, others can relate to your troubles. Second, if you need help, get it. Do not dare be embarrassed. Mental health used to be so taboo. People who received treatment at a hospital were considered "crazy" or "nuts." I have even heard someone coin the term of a mental health facility "the looney bin." And they were a worker, for goodness' sake. Get the help you need, trust the Lord, and love your family; everything will be manageable. Your darker days will be fewer, and your lighter days will shine brighter.

Made in the USA
Coppell, TX
31 December 2023

27082411R00108